STRONG AND COURAGEOUS

Joshua's Lessons for Athletes
(and the Cheering Section)

Kevin Vande Streek

with Wallace Bratt

Calvin College
Grand Rapids, MI 49546

Vande Streek, Kevin; Bratt, Wallace
Strong and Courageous: Joshua's Lessons for Athletes (and the Cheering Section)

Library of Congress Control Number: 2011929555

ISBN 978-0-9832385-0-8

Cover photo: Scott Hailstone, from iStockphoto

Have I not commanded you?
Be strong and courageous.
Do not be terrified;
do not be discouraged,
for the Lord your God
will be with you
wherever you go.

JOSHUA 1:9

CONTENTS

PREFACE

While growing up I was taught in the faith at home, church and school. I learned quickly of God's love and grace, of His gift of Jesus Christ, His call for salvation, and about how we are called to live our lives of service in response. I often tell teams that I have coached that we don't do devotions together so that God will help us win a game. Rather, it's so that we can stop for a moment and understand that our belief in Him and our living for Him applies to every area of our life, including something as insignificant as a basketball game.

A few years ago, Joel Boot, my pastor at Ridgewood Christian Reformed Church in Jenison, Mich., gave a sermon on a portion of the story of Joshua. I scribbled notes on the bulletin that would apply to my coaching and our team so that I could later use them in one of our devotional times. When I got home I read the entire book and was overwhelmed by how closely this story relates to the daily lives of coaches, players and fans.

Today's society has a severely distorted perspective of sports. I thought Joshua would be a great story to share the inspirational message of faith and to help us understand and demonstrate why and how we should play and live, and for whom we are playing and living. I hope our reflections on Joshua inspire you.

This book would not have become a reality without the tireless and heartfelt efforts of Calvin emeritus professor Wallace Bratt. Wally became a great encourager of my coaching and teaching efforts from the time I was hired at Calvin and continues to be an example of faith and light in my life, as he has been to thousands of people over the years. To work with him on this project has been a great blessing. I thank him as a friend and brother in Christ.

Others have played a role in this volume, too. Support and encouragement for my life and work come from my wife, Vicki; our four sons, K.C., Brian, Matthew and Daniel; Calvin president Gaylen Byker; Rev. Joel Boot; and Dr. Glen Van Andel. For work on the review of manuscripts I'd like to thank Susan Buist, Jennifer Penning, Lynn Rosendale and Gordon Van Harn. Thank you to Bob Alderink for the cover design and text layout. And finally I'd like to thank Mike Van Denend and the Calvin Alumni Association board for their efforts in the publication of *Strong and Courageous*.

WHY JOSHUA?

What does the ancient book of Joshua have to say to you as a Christian athlete today?

To begin with, this Old Testament book tells an amazing story. It narrates how that huge mass of Israelites, after 40 years of wandering in the desert, finally crossed the River Jordan in miraculous fashion; how they conquered Jericho and many other strongholds, though often heavily outnumbered; how they sometimes stumbled along the way and had lessons to learn, some of them bitter; and how after seven years of struggle they finally occupied the promised land and could begin to enjoy the results of their successful efforts. There's great adventure in what they do, as much as in any sports event you'll ever play in. Furthermore, you'll find that their ups and downs are in some ways yours, too.

Then there's Joshua himself, the one called by God to lead the Israelites into their new land, who is a wonderful role model in his faithfulness, levelheaded approach to leadership, ability to work with others as a team and strong sense of commitment. Other biblical narratives tell of leaders like King Saul, who started out strong but eventually fizzled out. That's not Joshua. He started strong and he finished strong, trusting his Lord all along the way. That's a goal for you as an athlete, too, isn't it— consistency and the ability, by God's grace, to finish strong in athletics and in all of your life?

Finally, the book of Joshua tells of God's encouragement in tough times and of His promises to be there every inch of the way. It's a story of His promise-keeping, whatever daunting situations

His people might face. What athlete, coach or spectator doesn't encounter obstacles at one time or another, and who among us can do without the encouragement and strength our Lord stands ready to give? The Joshua story is ultimately God's story, and it's a wonderful reminder that He never wants you to walk alone—not in any aspect of your life, including your sport.

So go for it, and give Joshua's example a chance to stiffen your backbone; to sensitize you to the needs of others and especially your teammates; to encourage you to live faithfully; and to be led closer toward a joy that's firmly grounded and will finally carry you through. Always.

CHALLENGES:

What goals do you have for yourself as an athlete, a Christian athlete?

What kinds of goals do you have for your team?

Which character trait in particular would you like to develop this season?

MOB SCENES AND LEADERSHIP

Exodus 3:1-10

Have you ever seen a mob scene, when a leaderless crowd of people rampages and is out of control? Unfortunately, it sometimes happens in university towns after a team wins (or loses) a national championship. The result is often smashed shop windows, burned cars, vandalism and arrests.

The Lord clearly did not want a mob scene as the Israelites left Egypt after decades of mistreatment and the resulting resentment. He had heard the cries of His people and had determined that it was time for their release, but there were, according to Exodus 12, well over a million of them. Talk about a mob! He knew that they needed a strong leader if their move to the Promised Land was to be successful. In this Bible passage from Exodus 3 the Lord chooses Moses for the tremendous task of providing that leadership.

It's that way today, isn't it? Any group needs effective leadership if it is to accomplish something meaningful. We obviously need God's leadership first of all. Without it, we will lose our sense of Kingdom purpose and produce little of value. His leadership always comes first. Always.

But He also uses men and women to serve as leaders in working out His Kingdom designs, leaders who follow His way.

As is true in all of life, athletic teams need leaders and leadership, too. Coaches are vital in providing a key part of it, but they will be the first to insist that leadership also must come from within their team. There must be players who serve as leaders by encouraging, setting an example and holding their teammates accountable. Without that kind of leadership, team chemistry will remain only a myth.

God shows in His choice of Moses that He doesn't need outstanding people to serve as leaders. He can use you, if you follow Him, prayerfully accepting for yourself the promise He gave Moses: "I will be with you."

Effective leaders need good followers, too. Not followers like the Israelites, who undercut Moses and blamed him when things went wrong. No, they need followers, teammates who support their leaders and make their suggestions for improvement gently and perhaps privately.

Good followers are leaders in their own right. In both life and athletics, they show their fellow players that the team comes first, that others come first, before their individual interests.

CHALLENGES:

Do you see yourself as a leader or a follower?

What's difficult about being a leader?

Why can it be tough to be a follower?

ME, A LEADER?

Exodus 3:11

When athletes are faced with the challenge of becoming a leader, they tend, in my experience, to respond in one of three ways.

Some greet the challenge with confidence. They're like politicians running for office. They're pretty sure they have what it takes to lead successfully, and they're chomping at the bit to get at it. They are comfortable feeling in charge and are gifted in relating to people and inspiring them.

If you have these characteristics, you probably should be careful. You should ask others whether they, too, think you have the right qualities for leadership. And you should analyze your own motives. Are you out to advance yourself or to lead for the good of the team?

Others don't want to stand out but are quietly willing to work behind the scenes as leaders. They'll get to know their teammates and will encourage and support them—and their coaches. Every team needs this kind of leadership to be successful. Joshua must have practiced it in the 40 years between his first spying mission and his eventual appointment as leader of the Israelites. At least he's never mentioned as being out front during those years. That role fell to Moses.

Then there's a third response, one that goes something like, "Who, me? You'd better look for someone else to lead. I'm not fit for the job. You don't know about my past, you don't know how I lived to break all the rules, how badly I messed up and sinned. You don't need defective, tainted people like me to lead."

Moses must have had some of the same thoughts as people in this third group when God confronted him in the burning bush. Maybe that's why he was reluctant when God called him to lead.

He seems to have had a bad temper, judging by the way he killed the Egyptian he saw beating one of the Israelites. Today it would be called a case of unpremeditated murder. Then he fled the scene of the crime, turned tail and ran in order to avoid prosecution. And all these actions surely did not show loyalty to Pharaoh's daughter, his adoptive mother. But God used him to lead anyway, despite his heavy load of sin baggage.

Always remember that if you've repented, God's forgiving grace is far greater than anything you may have done. Anything. You're forgiven and now can help others avoid the pitfalls that sidetracked your own life. You, too, may be called to lead.

CHALLENGES:

Do you fit into any of the categories listed above?

Could you be a leader if called to be one?

Is there anything standing in your way of becoming a leader?

DROPPING THE BATON

Joshua 1:1-9

Have you ever watched a relay race in which one of the runners dropped the baton, even though the person before him or her had passed it cleanly? Perhaps anxiety was at fault or over-eagerness to catch a leading runner from another team. In any case, a dropped baton meant the end of the race.

In today's passage, God calls Joshua to take the baton from Moses, to succeed him as leader of the Israelites. God knows that taking that baton and running with it is a huge job, a frightening job. That's why He encourages Joshua not to be terrified.

Joshua's life under God had prepared him for leadership. He had seen God's power during the 10 plagues in Egypt; he had shown trust in God's leadership when, together with Caleb, he gave his optimistic report after his scouting mission into the Promised Land many years before; and he had served as Moses' personal aide for some 40 years.

He must have seen the problems of leadership, too, when he witnessed how stubborn, faithless and difficult the Israelites could be.

Leadership in any area of life can be a challenge. In athletics, too. Leaders can be subject to envy, stubbornness and unfair criticism. But we're told that Joshua was at heart humble, not someone who relished power for the sake of his own ego. At the end of the book he is described as being a true servant leader.

Leadership can be a great adventure. But it's important to prepare yourself as best you can. If you wish to become a leader, it is vital that you be a thoughtful observer, that you get to know your teammates in various situations, listen to them, *look to the Lord for strength*, and then accept the baton as you step up and take responsibility.

And if you're a genuinely humble leader, like Joshua's predecessor Moses was, you also will train someone to eventually take your place, you'll encourage and help your successor on her or his way. Good leaders produce more leaders. You won't clutch power tightly in your hand, but you'll remember that your first concern is the good of the team, the well-being of the group. That's what servant leadership is about in all aspects of God's Kingdom, including athletics—and in your life, too.

CHALLENGES:

What characteristics mark the good leaders you've witnessed?

Why, in your experience, can a position of leadership also involve great temptations?

Have you seen leaders who are reluctant to relinquish their leadership? What happens when that is the case?

THE RIGHT STUFF

Joshua 1:6-9

In our last devotional we were reminded that leadership can be a great adventure, but the book of Joshua also reminds us that it can be a tough task. Three times in today's reading the Lord tells Joshua that he will need courage to fulfill his task. "Be strong and courageous," He says in both verses 6 and 9; in verse 7 the Lord intensifies that admonition, saying, "Be strong and very courageous." God, after all, promises to be with him. What more could you want?

What the Lord is asking of Joshua is trust. Trust me. And Joshua had trusted Him. When outnumbered 10 to two after his spying foray into Canaan, Joshua was one of two young men who showed courage born of trust as he spoke against majority opinion. Despite public opinion, he trusted the Lord's promises that Israel could prevail against the inhabitants of the Promised Land. It isn't easy to speak against the majority, but Joshua did it.

In sports, trust is the base of the leadership pyramid, a trust that runs both ways. Leaders in athletics are called to live lives, under God, that invite others to trust them, but they also must show trust in the teammates they are leading.

Trusting in both of those directions can be a tall order. It's easy to have suspicions about the trustworthiness of some of the people on the team. But trust can inspire trust. When you show trust in others, you're inviting them to trust you as well.

Without trust in coaches, team leaders and teammates, no team will ultimately succeed, whether it wins or loses on the scoreboard. It's that simple. That's especially true near the end of close contests, when you have to rely on teammates and the coach's plan.

And if in those situations you're a sub observing from poolside, the bench or the sidelines, your support of those actively competing is in a real way evidence of your trust in them and their ability to succeed. Mistrust will bring only anger, discouragement, hurt and finally spiritual collapse; teams have to trust if they're really to be teams.

Joshua trusted His Lord right on through to the end of his life. That's the kind of trust that serves as a sure foundation for our lives, too. That's why we're called to "trust the Lord with all our heart."

CHALLENGES:

Do you find it difficult to trust your coach and some of your teammates?

If that's the case, what should be done about it? What can you do about it?

Who needs more trust: starters or substitutes who wish they could be in the game?

ENCOURAGEMENT

Joshua 1:9

Major League Baseball has a long history of players with nicknames. Ryan Braun of the Brewers has been dubbed "The Hebrew Hammer" because of his Jewish heritage and ability to hit. Tampa Bay's Carl Crawford is called "The Perfect Storm" because of his rare combination of skills, and Derek Jeter of the Yankees has the nickname "Captain Clutch" because of his ability to perform in tight situations.

Do you have any friends with the nickname "Barnabas"? Probably not, for that New Testament name seems to have gone out of style. And it's too bad, for the name means, among other things, "Son of Encouragement," and encouragement is as necessary now as it was in Joshua's time. Everyone goes through dark valleys; it's just a question of when.

Encouragement may take plenty of different forms. Sometimes just showing up when you're needed is encouragement. Sometimes a smile or pat on the back will give a lift to someone in trouble. Sometimes even telling people they can do better is a form of building them up. The possibilities are endless, and the value of encouragement we give others can be greater than we'll ever imagine.

In today's text we read that the Lord encouraged Joshua at the outset of a huge undertaking: crossing the Jordan and defeating Jericho. But He didn't just say something like, "You can do it, I know you can." Instead He encouraged him by telling him, "the Lord your God will be with you wherever you go."

That's encouragement built on a solid foundation, and there's nothing phony about it.

Encouragement in athletics is of huge importance. When a teammate high-fives a volleyball player who has just served out of bounds or into the net, it speaks volumes. Among other things, it says, "we still need you, we know you can do it, we're with you, we respect you." And encouragement from the bench or from the stands makes all the difference in the world. Encouragement helps coaches and teachers, too.

Ultimately, the solid foundation on which our encouragement is based is the same as it was in Joshua's day: the Lord our God will be with us wherever we go and whatever challenges, sorrows or failures we face—in our lives as young athletes, too. If we really believe that, we have every reason to build up one another.

When we encourage others with their best interests at heart and out of Christian love, we are speaking God's language and the language of His people. And that's not a foreign language to any of us who want to live for Him.

CHALLENGES:

When have you been helped by someone else's encouragement of you?

In what ways can you encourage others?

Do you get encouragement from your faith? When and why?

TALK TO ME

Joshua 2:1-14

I t's the same old story, isn't it? Parents stop talking with one another or with their kids. Sons or daughters give each other, friends or parents the silent treatment because of some real or imagined hurt. Old friends, perhaps in their 60s, maybe even fellow church members, suddenly quit talking to one another. And when talk stops, it's a sure sign of trouble.

Speech, the ability to talk, is a huge gift from our Lord. We often don't realize it until something goes badly wrong. Maybe it's a severely autistic child we know who's totally locked within herself. Maybe it's a grandparent who's had a stroke and can no longer speak. Maybe it's a friend so depressed that she or he can't even talk. Whatever the cause, at times like that we realize how vital speech is to who we are.

Speech in itself can be destructive, of course. Speech without love, according to the Apostle Paul, is nothing but a clanging cymbal. On the other hand, talk becomes easy when we trust each other, as our Lord calls us to do. James says that we are to trust so fully that we are even able to confess our sins to one another.

Athletic teams need both trust and the talk that naturally flows from it. It's a two-way street: Wholesome, effective communication breeds trust and trust breeds communication. Coach K, the enormously successfully basketball coach at Duke University, considers communication so important that he ranks it right up there with learning the system of defense and the system of offense as one of the three key aspects of his coaching system.

It's important that players feel free to talk to their coaches and their fellow teammates. You can't function as a team if there are pent-up hostilities that block the way of good talk. Words of encouragement, on the other hand, are a vital form of support and community building.

Sometimes speech can even be a lifesaver. In today's reading, Rahab opened her heart to the spies and told them of her great fear. In her precarious situation she understood the vital importance of speech. If she had not spoken, she most likely would have perished along with her fellow citizens when Jericho's "walls came tumblin' down." Her speech ultimately saved the day for herself and her family.

Never forget that to speak in love is to truly speak "in the tongues of men and angels."

CHALLENGES:

Do you know any people who have stopped talking to one another? What happens when icy silence sets in?

Have you ever seen friends or teammates who quit talking to each other? If you have, what were the results?

Is there anyone with whom you should be talking and thereby building bridges? Think about it.

How can you lead and build team unity with your speech?

STOP AND LISTEN

Joshua 3:9

Afew years ago I was privileged to spend an afternoon with John Wooden, perhaps the most successful college basketball coach of the 20th century. Over a 12-year span at UCLA, his teams won a total of 10 NCAA national championships. Coach Wooden lived a long life, dying in 2010 at the age of nearly 100.

Wooden was a Christian. If he were writing this devotional on Joshua 3:9, he probably would stress at least two things. For one, he would have agreed on the necessity of Joshua's call to the Israelites to stop and listen before crossing the Jordan, to listen to the word of the Lord.

Our culture is a busy one, sometimes too busy to stop and listen. Your life is probably that way, too. School, practice, homework, a part-time job and friends make tremendous demands on your time. Who has time to stop and listen? Even Sunday worship sometimes tends to take a back seat in our scheduling.

But those worship services are important, even vital to our spiritual health. It's terribly important that we stop at least once a week and listen to the word of the Lord. If we blindly charge into a new week without pausing to worship and meditate and evaluate, we will eventually lose our way, which must be the Lord's way.

Stopping and paying attention are key activities in athletics, too. One of Coach Wooden's more notable quotations is "Be quick, don't hurry." In sports as in our Christian lives, it's important not to rush into a situation and force a bad play. But when the situation warrants action, quickly take advantage of it. Don't dawdle or be half-hearted about it. Go for it.

John Wooden also understood a second reason why it is necessary for Christian athletes to stop, listen and evaluate: without doing so we will lose perspective. This Hall of Fame player and coach was blunt about it. "I have always made it clear that basketball [or any sport] is not the ultimate," he wrote. "There is only one life that truly wins, and that is the one that places faith in the hands of the Savior."

Vince Lombardi, former coach of the Green Bay Packers, is reported to have said, "Winning isn't everything; it's the only thing." He was right, although he may not have known it. It all depends on whose race you are running. Coach Wooden reminds us whose race truly matters.

CHALLENGES:

Do you have trouble keeping your sport in perspective?

How can you work at doing so?

WHO'S NUMBER ONE?

Joshua 3:10-13

Some of us like to plan; some of us just like to take it as it comes. What about you?

There's a peril with planning some aspects of our lives too precisely, of course. There's a lot of truth in the old saying, "Man proposes but God disposes." All sorts of things can happen along the way that can ruin our plans, and that can be frustrating.

However, teams need to do some planning if they are to function well. In today's reading, Joshua had precise plans about how the Israelites were to cross the Jordan. Orders were given to the people about how to behave, when to move forward, and how to keep a distance between themselves and the ark.

The most important thing about those plans, however, was basic and simple: They were to follow the Ark of the Covenant, which had to lead in that long procession. God had to come first.

That's the challenge for each of us, isn't it? To plan our hours, days and lives with God in first place. Conditioning, improving skills and developing game plans are important in sports, but honoring God first in all of our lives—in our everyday routines, in athletics, friendships and academics—is our highest calling. That's the key part of your plan that will bring you not only challenges and struggle, but also joy, hope and peace.

There's a reason for great hope when you plan with God first: God loves you. What He said to the exiled Israelites in Jeremiah 29:11 He also says to you: "For I know the plans I have for you … plans to prosper you and not to harm you, plans to give you hope and a future."

Now *that's* something solid you can plan on. Now and for all eternity.

CHALLENGES:

Is planning important to you? Why or why not?

What do you plan?

Have you, as an athlete, seen the consequences of poor planning? What were they?

Can planning too carefully be a sign of uncertainty or a lack of faith?

What tends to happen when we fail to put the Lord first? Who or what then takes His place?

CROSSING THE JORDAN SCARED

Joshua 3:14-17, 4:10-13

Thus far we've thought primarily about leadership and less about being a good follower. But being a follower in one sense can be a scary thing. It can demand tremendous faith and courage.

Think of those ordinary Israelites as they crossed the Jordan on dry ground. As they walked across the dry river bottom, do you think they wondered whether that piled-up water would let go and wash them to their deaths? There's one clue that this might well be the case. Note in chapter 4, verse 10, that the people "hurried over." I'd probably hurry, too. Wouldn't you?

We're sometimes like those Israelites. Of course, they had God's promise that they would make it safely through, but so do we. Yet when we're faced with tough situations—whether in sports, in schoolwork, in friendships, in college choice, in the illness of a parent, in family breakdown or any other problem—it requires great faith and courage to see things through, to make it to the far bank of the Jordan.

Prayer can help. Reading and memorizing scripture passages can give us courage to go on. So can taking time to remember God's mighty deeds in times past. So can being open with other Christians, young or old, about the struggles we're facing and asking them for their prayers and advice.

Life *can* be scary. Anyone who maintains that the Christian life is a piece of cake hasn't really been living. The Psalms are full of lament about life's trials and faith tested. And the Apostle Paul had plenty of whiplash scars on his back to prove that walking the Christian walk can hurt.

Athletics can bring challenges, too. They may include injury, the fear of being cut, riding the bench when you're sure you should be playing, bad publicity, disagreeable opponents, the envy of teammates, or the demands of training and practice. You know the challenges in your sport.

They do matter to your Lord. Though He is "the mighty God," great beyond what we can imagine, those worries are not too small for Him to care about. He's promised to be with you through your personal Jordans, if you rely fully on Him. His arms are strong, and His promises are sure.

CHALLENGES:

What challenging situations exist in your life?

Have you had experiences of the Lord's seeing you safely through dark times? Will He now?

IT'S NOT (JUST)
ABOUT YOU

Joshua 4:1-9

God surely deals with us as individuals with personal responsibilities and individual needs, but He also created us to be in community. As children of God we're members of one worldwide, overarching community, His church. But often, in athletics as in life, we're also placed in smaller, closely knit groups. A team is called to be one such community.

Human beings need one another. We can't become who God intends us to be without community. People who claim to be self-made never really are. Many other people have played a role in their development, such as parents, teachers, youth pastors and friends. If we are to fulfill our calling we need our Lord and we need one another. The story of the 12-stone memorial points us toward that truth.

Joshua, the strong leader, could have ignored God's instructions and carried those 12 stones from the middle of the river himself, afterward simply telling the Israelites what the memorial meant. But that wasn't God's way and it wasn't Joshua's way.

Instead he appointed one member from each of the 12 tribes to fetch those stones and bring them to the designated spot. Only after each tribe had made its contribution in that way did Joshua arrange the stones to form the memorial to the Lord's saving faithfulness.

In obedience to his God, Joshua did not call attention to himself. He wanted the people to know that this was a community project. A community responsibility. A community opportunity.

The same thing is true of teams, isn't it? Each member is to make her or his contribution; only then can unity develop as we recognize and rejoice in one another's gifts. Only then will our athletic community become a Christian community as well, a fellowship knit together in fun, gratitude and praise. And not so incidentally, it will also become a community that has a chance at success in every meaningful sense of the word.

CHALLENGES:

What do you do when one team member's contributions far outshine those of the others and thus are a potential threat to unity?

How can a team leader, perhaps a star player, avoid calling all the attention to herself or himself?

Do you really believe that each member has something to contribute to your team?

How do you help and encourage someone whose role is less visible and who therefore is reluctant to offer his or her contributions or suggestions?

POWER

Joshua 4:1-9

I n athletics, strength plus speed equals power. It can be seen in a shot putter, a diver, a hockey slap shot or a volleyball spike, just to name a few.

The word "power" has become popular in our culture. There are power drinks, power bars, powerhouses, power suits, power struggles, powerful sermons and even power naps. Power is something many people apparently find desirable, even crave.

Power in and of itself is neutral. Everything depends on how it is used. One person or community may be a power for evil, another a power for good. Hitler had power grounded in evil, but Mother Teresa had a blessed power all her own.

God's divine power definitely is not neutral. On occasion He may use it to punish, but the thrust of His power is ultimately to save, to deliver, to redeem. The writer of Psalm 62 had it right: "One thing God has spoken, two things have I heard: that you, O God, are strong, and that you, O Lord, are loving." Power used in love is what it's all about.

In the book of Joshua we are forcefully reminded of that loving power. In springtime at flood stage, when conditions were at their worst, with the Egyptians hot on their heels, God parted the Jordan River so that His people could pass through unharmed. This was only one instance of His strength, of course. The entire history of Israel shows Him to be a God mighty in power, mighty to save.

Most likely you, too, have faced your own Jordan, roadblocks on your way, obstacles that seemed too great to overcome. Maybe your team has faced them. Our tendency in such situations is to either despair or to try to plan our way past them.

But God invites us to a take a better way: to plan *and* to call on Him, the God who is mighty to save, at all times, and especially when the going gets tough. That goes for athletics, too, whether it be situations that arise in soccer, baseball, volleyball, golf or any other sport.

Relying on that loving power can bring about unexpected, often amazing results, even when His answer to our request is not what we wished for. He is, after all, God the Father Almighty.

CHALLENGES:

Have you heard of any recent, down-to-earth evidences of God's power in a difficult situation?

How do you instinctively respond when you face seemingly impossible situations?

How do you handle it when God finds it best not to use His power on your behalf?

INVESTING YOURSELF

Joshua 5:2-8

Commitments are easy to make, in a sense, but sometimes hard to keep. This also is true among professional athletes, like Tiger Woods, who broke his marriage commitment in spectacular fashion. His sin became public—but lest we become self-righteous, Jesus reminds us that we can even break a marriage commitment with our eyes, by the way we look at another person.

What is commitment, anyway? In its deeper biblical meaning it involves making a pledge, a promise. After the ark landed on dry ground, God made a commitment never again to cut off life by the waters of a flood. The visible sign of that commitment was the rainbow brightening the refreshed earth.

Embedded in that meaning of commitment is the idea of giving yourself. John 3:16 is about commitment, isn't it? In that text we are told that God committed Himself to the world so fully that He gave the supreme gift, His only Son, that He actually gave of Himself.

On a human level, when Ruth committed herself to Naomi she gave herself fully, pledging to stick with her wherever she went, in life and in death, even vowing to make Naomi's God her God.

In today's short reading, God reaffirmed His commitment to Israel through the rite of circumcision. In it He again laid claim to His delivered people, the people He promised to keep as His own. He invested Himself in them.

The Israelites, for their part, were thereby challenged to take ownership of this commitment by keeping God's commandments, by loving Him with all their heart, mind and soul. By committing themselves to Him. By giving themselves to Him. By putting Him first.

After the establishment of trust and communication, making commitments is the next stage in a team-building pyramid.* Christian athletes commit themselves first to their Lord, then to their team. Such athletes give themselves over to the group, pledging to make their own wishes secondary, to work first for the good of the team. And giving in that sense doesn't mean loss. As St. Francis said, it is in giving that we receive—in sports, too, and in all of life.

CHALLENGES:

Why is it hard to place the well-being of the group before our own wishes?

What will you and your team commit to?

How does putting the team first help build morale and unity?

What do you get in return when you give yourself to the team?

*See *The Five Dysfunctions of a Team* by Patrick Lencioni.

PASS THE AMMUNITION

Joshua 5:11-12

During World War II, which some of your grandparents or great-grandparents still remember, there was a popular song that ran, "Praise the Lord and pass the ammunition, and we'll all stay free." Church folk back then weren't sure about the appropriateness of that song, finding it somewhat flippant, but it did contain a real measure of biblical truth.

We find a similar truth in today's passage and in the entire story of the Israelites moving into the Promised Land. As long as they wandered in that barren desert, where crops could not be grown, they had to rely totally on the Lord for their food. But as soon as they reached the land God gave them, He expected them to get out there, to forage, to raise their own food, although it obviously was necessary that they continue to trust Him as well.

Trust and hard work go together. It is important to both "praise the Lord and pass the ammunition."

I suspect you'd find it quite bizarre if your coach said that this year your team was not going to practice for its games, but would instead meet every day for 90 minutes of prayer. Opponents would feast on you, your win-loss record would be dismal, and you wouldn't leave the season feeling satisfied.

In athletics, as in all of life, prayer is not an alternative to preparation, and faith is not a substitute for hard work. If our Lord felt that it was, He wouldn't bother telling us how we ought to live our everyday lives as we work for His Kingdom. Already in the Garden of Eden He told us to go out and cultivate the earth. Paradise was a place of both activity and a close walk with God.

It's hard to keep a balance in our Christian living, which includes our lives as athletes. It's so easy to think we're in charge, and if we don't get out there and do it, it won't be done at all. It's easy to forget to trust.

We need both trust and effort. It's not a question of one or the other. We practice, we work, trusting the Lord to bless our effort done in His name.

That's our Lord's formula for meaningful life.

CHALLENGES:

Where do you fall short: in trusting or in working hard?

What steps can you take to improve in each?

WINNING BEFORE
THE GAME STARTS

Joshua 5:13–6:5

As a kid, I played a Little League exhibition game inside the walls of a maximum-security prison in Waupun, Wisconsin. That was a unique experience.

But usually, when we think of walls, structures like the Great Wall of China come to mind. More recently there was also the Berlin Wall, intended, Communist politicians claimed, to protect the East Germans from the presumably hostile West. Humankind seems to like to build walls in times of threat and danger.

Today's passage tells of Jericho, a walled city, a strong fortress. Rahab and her countrymen already knew of the might of the Israelites' God. He had shown His power over nature by parting the Red Sea and His power over foreign hosts by defeating Sihon and Og, kings of the Amorites. But what about a walled city; would He be able to overcome that obstacle, too?

The Israelites themselves had to wonder about that wall. However, it was as though God anticipated their fears, for He told them even before they started that He had already delivered Jericho into their hands. In short, the battle was essentially over before it began.

The New Testament says something similar. It tells us that the war between the Lord's Kingdom and the satanic Kingdom of darkness also has been decided. Skirmishes may remain, tough battles that test God's people profoundly, but the final outcome is sure.

The certainty of that ultimate triumph has to quiet our fears, too. Though the evil so prominent in our world threatens to sweep Christ's Kingdom away, it will not ultimately win out. The battle has already been won in Christ our Lord.

That awareness gives us perspective in our personal lives, as we struggle against the devil in our daily walk, a struggle that can be intensely difficult. But the Lord has promised to see us through. He has won the final victory for us. Now it's a matter of walking close to Him, of following in His way.

It gives us perspective in another way, too. Whether we as athletes win or lose a crucial match or game, Christ's victory in the larger, more important battle is finally what really counts. Though we surely play to win, a lost athletic contest is not the end of the world. In fact, the end of the world promises to be a gateway to something far better and more glorious than the greatest upset we can ever pull off.

CHALLENGES:

Do you see any evidence that Christ has already won the battle?

Do you as an athlete have trouble keeping perspective when you lose—or win?

What do you find tougher: to be a good winner or a good loser? Why?

KNOCKING DOWN WALLS

Joshua 6:6-20

Sometimes walls decay slowly due to exposure to the weather; sometimes people tear them down. But none ever came down in such startling fashion as did the wall around Jericho. The way that wall fell is important, for it gives us at least three crucial insights into how we are to live our own lives before God.

First, it reminds us that the God who toppled Jericho's wall is both strong and dependable. He created the world, sustains it and sent His Son to redeem it. While on earth, that Son lived a perfect life, healed the sick, fed the hungry and raised the dead. Knowing of His loving power, you can be confident that He can handle anything you will ever face.

Second, this passage indicates that God expects us to take part in working out His will. He didn't allow the Israelites to simply sit quietly in their tents and wait. He commanded them to march, march and then march some more. They had to commit themselves to the task, just as the Lord expects us to decide which problems we are called to tackle, ask for help when we need it and work to carry out the part of the job that is ours. Prayer is vital, financial assistance is often necessary, but nothing replaces personal commitment to a project.

And third, this passage is a reminder of the source of our gifts—the Lord God who made, equipped and redeems us. The Israelites realized where their strength came from, thanked the Lord for it and devoted the conquered city to Him. None of them made the "we're No. 1" sign, nor did they go about boasting of what they had done. Their behavior, at least for now, is a shining reminder of who ultimately must get the credit for their glorious victory.

Winning brings its own temptations, doesn't it? Pride, cockiness and excessive self-confidence are but a few. While achieving a hard-fought victory against great odds ought to make us exuberantly happy and maybe even give us a "high," we can enrich those feelings with our gratitude to the Lord who gave us the healthy bodies and alert minds that helped make it all possible.

CHALLENGES:

Do your opponents sometimes irritate you? Why?

What means can the Lord use to sometimes stifle our pride and help us come back "down to earth"?

What can build walls between teammates?

Why do effective leadership and team chemistry depend on those walls tumbling down?

ROLLING YOUR EYES

Joshua 2:17-21, 6:22-25

Have you ever caught yourself rolling your eyes when a parent or friend says something you find totally out of line? Have you seen others do it? When you're rolling your eyes, you're not speaking one word, but you're telling those around you that you find some word, attitude or action to be ridiculous, even bizarre.

There are many other ways of expressing yourself without using speech. Sometimes they're helpful and positive. Tears of gratitude carry a message. A smile can do it, as will an encouraging pat on the back, squeezing someone's hand or a high-five. And the list goes on.

Wordless communication can also convey a negative message. Looking away when someone's trying to talk to you probably indicates you could care less. A frown will do it. Teeth clenched in anger can do it. Unfortunately, so will an obscene hand gesture.

Speech is vital for effective communication and for building trust. But nonverbal communication, a message conveyed without words, also matters. It can matter a lot.

In today's reading, Rahab uses nonverbal communication to save her own life and the lives of family members. That red cord says, among other things, "I'm expecting you former spies to keep your word. I'm *waiting* for you to come through. We're keeping our end of the bargain. How about you?"

Wordless communication is very powerful in sports. In fact, it's hard to overestimate its importance.

Hanging your head when you come out of a game and going straight to the end of the bench or line without accepting a high-five from a teammate says volumes and hurts morale. It also threatens to damage relationships.

On the other hand, pointing to the person who made a good pass, patting the back of a player who messed up, helping another player off the floor builds morale, strengthens relationships and creates a positive environment. Try it; you'll see for yourself.

CHALLENGES:

Name five ways of communicating without words.

When you "speak without talking," are you usually "saying" something positive or negative?

When can nonverbal communication sometimes be more helpful than using words?

A WALK-ON WITH
A SHADY PAST

Joshua 2:1, 6:22-25

The sports pages of newspapers like to play it up big when a walk-on, someone who was not recruited or granted a scholarship, plays so well that he or she not only makes the team but is granted a "full-ride" scholarship.

Rahab, in a sense, was that kind of person, a walk-on, someone who wasn't on the preseason Israelite roster. First, she was not one of the chosen people and had not been recruited by Joshua to help the spies escape. And second, she also was a prostitute, which placed her still further outside the ranks of the Israelites.

But God used her anyway, as she helped the spies avoid capture so that they could give their encouraging report to Joshua. Because of the vital role she had played, she and her family were spared when the walls of Jericho fell and were given a place to live among the Israelites. She had made her contribution, and God blessed her in a unique way when the rest of her countrymen were destroyed.

The story of Rahab reminds us that God doesn't use only the cream of the crop as he builds His Kingdom here on earth. That's a huge comfort for so many of us who feel we're just ordinary or even below average. It's also a comfort for those of us burdened with past sins and failures. God can work through our faults and around them. Look how he used Rahab.

God may sometimes choose the brightest and the best, but often He does not. God may sometimes call the pure in heart for His purposes, but sometimes He uses those whose past is a mess. He eventually reshapes them, but first He takes them just as they are. After all, He's notable for both His power and His love.

It's an example for us as teammates, too. God doesn't care whether we're the most or least talented player on the team. He can use us in whatever role he assigns us. And He's not put off by our messy pasts, either. Never forget that in athletics or in any part of your life.

In a sense, we're all walk-ons. Way back in Eden we chose to distance ourselves from God, to walk away, but through the death and glorious resurrection of our Lord Jesus Christ we can rejoin His family and be welcomed to His team.

That's pretty great news, isn't it?

CHALLENGES:

Have you seen persons not accepted because of their reputation or past?

How do you feel God can use you, in spite of your past errors?

Do you find it hard to accept people who have been a disgrace to you or others?

BEING ACCOUNTABLE

Joshua 7:1-26

A second pile of rocks appeared on the landscape, this one radically different from the first one in what it signified. The first was a memorial to God's bringing the Israelites safely through the Jordan; the second was a reminder of one man's disobedience in the face of God's very explicit command. It was a sign that the Lord held the perpetrator, Achan, accountable for his sin.

When the Israelites swept into Jericho, everyone but one person obeyed the command to stay away from the things devoted to the treasury of the Lord's house: the silver and gold they found and the articles of bronze and iron. That one man was Achan, who secretly took forbidden items and buried them beneath the floor of his tent.

The concept of a victimless crime, as it is sometimes used today, is a myth. Somebody always gets hurt. The loving heart of our Lord is one sure victim, as His will gets trampled on. Obviously, Achan's family suffered terribly, too, but beyond that, as is often so true, the entire community was affected by his sin. The Lord withdrew from Israel as they went overconfidently into battle, and they lost decisively. After Joshua learned who the culprit was, Achan and his family had to die before the Lord's favor returned to the camp.

All of us obviously are accountable to the Lord. But we're also accountable to our community, whether it be large or small, for our actions affect it, too. Sometimes things we do hurt the people we love and respect most of all. Practicing accountability also suggests that we are responsible *for* one another, that we are called to hold one another to account for their good and the good of the community.

That's true in dealing with teammates, too, isn't it? Of course, to call others to account in selfish, condescending or self-righteous fashion is only to add one sin to the other. Instead, we are expected to speak to one another in love and concern, with a view to helping our teammates in their Christian walk.

That takes courage, of course. But after we've developed real trust, communication and commitment, it will be possible to both give and receive such correction with grace. And the entire team, the entire community will profit from it—including you.

CHALLENGES:

Why is it tough to hold others to account?

Are you willing to be held accountable by a teammate?

How does the entire team, the entire community, benefit from such openness?

Why do you think a coach asks for evaluations of his or her work at the end of the season?

OVERCONFIDENCE
AND PRIDE

Joshua 7:3-7

Overconfidence and pride can kill you when it comes to sports. Those traits routinely cause upsets and throw national rankings into confusion. In 1983 the 10-loss Wolfpack of North Carolina State defeated the 32-1 Houston Cougars for the NCAA basketball championship. In 2007 it was little Appalachian State beating the mighty, fifth-ranked University of Michigan in football for perhaps the biggest upset in college football history. Who knows what it will be this year?

In today's passage the Israelites appear to have suffered from that same sense of overconfidence. The scouts who spied upon the city of Ai confidently reported that the Israelites need not assemble a full army to conquer it. A mere handful of troops could take care of the job. No sweat.

It was only after they were defeated that they came to their senses. Even Joshua couldn't determine what had happened, although he sensed that he had to immediately call on the Lord to find some answers. Even he had to be reminded that if the Lord was not on Israel's side, failure would result.

Confidence is important in the Christian life—the confidence that comes from deep-down belief that the Lord is in control and will work His will in our lives. It gives us the grace and boldness to move ahead with each new day.

It's important in sports, too. Cross country runners who lack confidence won't dare to move out strong if they aren't confident in their ability to also finish strong. A soccer goalie who isn't confident will hesitate when it comes to moving out of the net when it's necessary, and the ball may whiz past him for a goal. A basketball player who hesitates to take that final shot in a tight game will find that the clock has run out and her team has lost. You can add to these examples a host of your own.

But if we let pride and overconfidence take over, in one way or another we'll fall on our faces, and those cuts and bruises hurt. That's the way God's world works. Teams in the middle of a long win streak need humility and prayer just as much as teams with a losing record. Maybe they need it more.

That goes for individuals, too. Outstanding athletes need gratitude to their Lord who gave them their talents, rather than a selfish pride that turns off everyone else and damages their own spiritual lives.

The Bible is clear in reminding us that pride goes before a fall. It also tells us that being thankful is God's antidote to pride.

And it works—and brings the right kind of joy and confidence with it, a confidence based on trusting the Lord and His love.

CHALLENGES:

Do you have to fight a tendency toward self-centered pride?

How do you keep overconfidence from hurting your team?

AND THE
WINNER IS . . . ?

Joshua 8:1-23

Developing strategy can have at least two purposes. On the one hand, it can be an attempt to go it on our own, to force our own will through, without reference to God. That kind of strategy may be successful for the moment, but in the long run it is an expression of human pride and is an offense to the Lord.

However, devising a strategy can also be a prayerful way of using the resources the Lord has given us in the best possible way, remembering that it is He who gives us the ability to come up with a way of meeting a challenge and that the victory ultimately is His.

When the Lord told the people of Israel to proceed on Ai, He clearly expected His servant Joshua to use his mind, to develop a plan for achieving the defeat of the city.

So Joshua worked out a strategy of ambush that proved to be immensely effective. After Ai's army was lured out of the city, the Israelites lying in wait entered and took it. The ensuing action, a kind of pincer maneuver, resulted in the total destruction of the city. But Joshua knew in advance that it was finally the Lord who would win the victory. Lest he forget that vital fact, the Lord Himself reminded him, as we read in verse 18.

Planning and strategizing are also important in sports. It's important to have a plan and to commit yourself to it, both individually and as a team. Without it you will waste your conditioning, your practice, and your physical and mental resources. And it's important to follow through on what you've planned.

Sometimes strategies have to be changed or adjusted to meet changing circumstances. But that's OK. The need for a plan remains.

Yet it is vital to remember that the Lord finally is in control, and that His finally is the Kingdom, the power and the glory; He is in charge, and you may be certain that He will use your plans in ways that best serve His loving purposes for you, your teammates and your coaches. But he expects you to plan, to use the resources He has given you wisely. To do so is to your benefit, too.

CHALLENGES:

How do you take it when your best plans—or your team's—seem to go haywire?

Do you find it hard to adapt to changing strategies, changing plans? Why or why not?

What happens when people try to ram their plans through, come what may?

EVERYDAY
THANKSGIVING

Joshua 8:30-31

Saying "thank you" does not come naturally. Parents of young children will be the first to tell you so. Saying "please" may come more easily, as it may be a gateway for asking for something a child wants. But making the words "thank you" a regular part of a little boy or girl's vocabulary is another thing. And it's not just small children who forget to say it. Older students and adults forget, too.

The culture in which we live is often termed a culture of entitlement. That's a fancy way of saying that we tend to think we have things coming to us. Athletes, especially the pros, can be glaring examples of such an attitude.

Because they are good at tennis or baseball or football, they assume the world owes them something special, and they pout when they don't get it, be it admiration, respect or ridiculously high wages. Anyone who lives that way, not just athletes, is not likely to grow hoarse from saying "thank you."

Joshua's building of an altar in today's reading shows that he thought differently. He knew that whatever the Israelites achieved was a gift from their Lord and that it deserved recommitment, praise, celebration, devotion and gratitude. His making sacrifice to the Lord on behalf of the people was, among other things, an expression of thanksgiving for the Lord's faithfulness in again delivering His people after the battle for Ai.

When any group, including members of a team, learns to say thanks, a whole new culture, a new spirit develops. It's an attitude of friendliness, gratitude, appreciation and even joy. It's a confidence builder and a recognition that we need one another and are thankful that the other person is there.

Our Lord deserves an entire life lived in gratitude to Him, of course. He has given us all we are and all we have, and it's vital to remember that. But to also thank teammates, coaches, and even officials and opponents—to say nothing of parents—is to brighten the entire atmosphere and even to bring the Kingdom of God one step closer. And it's never too late to start.

CHALLENGES:

When was the last time you thanked your parents?

Is it possible to be thankful, to say thanks, even when you've just lost a tough match or contest?

Jesus regularly gave thanks to the Father. Why can it be so hard for us to be thankful persons?

What people in your life are you thankful for?

TRICKY OPPOSITION, TRICKY TEMPTATIONS

Joshua 9:1-27

Wthat is easier for you to deal with in your Christian life: direct opposition or opposition that is indirect, more subtle? In today's reading we see both types. The military opposition of the coalition of six kings was a head-on threat to God's people, while the Gibeonites used deceit and trickery to disarm Joshua's forces.

Direct opposition to Christ's Kingdom has many faces today. It may come in the form of political candidates who publicly sneer at the name of Jesus (this has happened); it may also be seen in the development of policies that disregard the sanctity of human life or the rights of the poor.

On a personal level it can involve the intentional use of profanity in your presence or a mocking response to your identifying yourself as a Christian in the place where you hold a part-time job. Or it can be direct pressure by non-Christian friends to use drugs or alcohol and thus compromise your faith.

Subtler opposition also has many faces and may be harder to detect. It comes in the form of popular movies that play fast and loose with sex and marriage, or popular songs that assume or even glorify an objectionable lifestyle without directly saying so. Or maybe it's a troubled close friend who hints that she really wants to "use" your homework. Or maybe it's the desire to be "cool" in the eyes of your friends, regardless of what it costs in terms of your faith.

Christian athletes, too, face many forms of opposition and temptation. There's the temptation to "pay back" an opponent who has roughed you up. It occurs when you exhibit an attitude that regards opposing team members as enemies, not as opponents. You could slack off when your coach isn't around or join in the criticism of another teammate or coach in order to be "in." You might make an idol of your sport without even realizing it.

Christian friends or parents can often help you identify these subtler forms of opposition when you don't notice them. But one thing is sure: We are called to oppose those things that threaten our Christian walk—not so that we can put on a phony halo or be arrogant, but so that God's name is praised, people around us are strengthened and our own lives may know real happiness, the happiness God wants for us.

CHALLENGES:

Why is there a temptation to see members of the other team as enemies?

How should a Christian team or athlete be different? Think about it.

What are the worst opponents against your Christian walk?

Will you have the courage to not allow direct or indirect opposition by your teammates?

THE TROUBLE
WITH TROUBLE

Joshua 10:1-8

Trouble sometimes comes alone, but often as twins—and sometimes as triplets or quadruplets, or worse still, as quintuplets. That was Joshua's situation. In today's reading, he faced five troubles simultaneously in five hostile kings and their armies. The odds were grim, but Joshua met this multiple enemy in confidence and trust, and in the Lord's strength he defeated it.

Nobody goes through life without trouble—not the richest pop stars in the country, not the greatest sprinter or swimmer, not the smartest kid for miles around.

Some people excel at hiding their problems, but be assured that problems exist. Since the fall in the Garden of Eden, troubles grow like weeds that can choke out even the potentially healthiest flowers in the garden or crops in the field. They can become our enemies and drain our energies. They can cause us to wilt and hang our heads.

You're in good company if you, too, have problems all your own—sometimes big ones. It may be difficulties with schoolwork. It may be one of your teachers. It may be family issues. It may be girl problems or boy problems. It may be a disagreement with your coach or trouble with friends or facing opponents who haven't lost a game all year. It might be some menacing combination of the above. Who knows? Problems have many faces.

How should we respond?

You work at those challenges, of course, and try to seek advice in your struggles. Friends, sometimes older people, including your parents or coaches, can be a great source of strength, as well as your pastors or church youth group leaders. But ultimately it comes down to trust, trust in the Lord who, sometimes contrary to appearances, always means well for you.

Perhaps the greatest gift you can return to the Lord is your trust in Him. Did you ever think of it that way? He longs for your trust. And in return for it, He can strengthen your backbone, refresh your wilted spirits and see you through it all.

That's how Joshua behaved: in trust. And the Lord enabled him to overcome. That's what He promises to do for you, too. Try Him, and you'll see.

CHALLENGES:

What are some tempting but harmful ways to get past your problems?

Why is it tempting to try to solve problems yourself rather than to give them over to God?

Does adversity depress you or motivate you to achieve?

How can you help your friends whose troubles seem too heavy to bear?

THE DAY THE SUN STOOD STILL

Joshua 10:1-14

D o you ever wish the days were longer? Maybe when a combination of a long, tiring practice, chores you are expected to do at home, the demands of friendship and time-consuming homework makes you wonder how you'll cram everything into one day.

It's a problem at least as old as Joshua, who saw that the day wasn't going to be long enough for the Israelites to finish defeating the enemy coalition they faced. He had such trust in the Lord that he literally called a miracle into being, as the Lord held the sun in its place for some 24 hours, until the Israelites were able to conquer their enemies. Whether the Lord manipulated the sun's rays, slowed the earth's rotation or used some other means, the fact remains that He performed a great miracle.

Even though God still works miracles, sometimes in the form of unexplained healings, for example, He doesn't normally intervene in the workings of the sun and stars any longer. Still, we can learn from what happened on the day of that fateful battle.

When Joshua saw the need Israel's army had, he didn't panic or become frantic. Instead, he called on the Lord, trusting that His help would be sufficient. And it was. Prayer does change things. Even today the Lord does "listen to a man [or woman]," as our passage puts it.

We can also learn from the unnamed narrator of the story. When the battle was over, he reminded us that "surely the Lord was fighting for Israel!" He gave credit to whom all credit was due.

That's true of all of the victories we win in our lives. They're all finally of God's doing. We work hard, practice hard, play hard and sometimes win tough games. And we can be happy and even proud when we come out winners. But finally, it's the Lord who gave us the strength to do it.

Acknowledging the real victor in it all is an expression of gratitude. And on a different level, if we should lose, giving credit to the team that won also shows an attitude worthy of athletes claimed by Christ.

CHALLENGES:

Have there been any minor (or major) miracles in your life or the life of your family?

Are you subject to panic attacks? Do you really believe that prayer makes a difference?

KEEPING YOUR WORD

Joshua 10:5-7

Try this one. A friend or acquaintance asks you to promise something. You make the promise, and later the friend asks you to keep that promise. You've learned in the meantime that she or he lied to you when asking you to make the original pledge. Would you still feel bound to keep it, or would you feel off the hook, since your friend lied to you in the first place?

Joshua didn't feel that the deceit of the Gibeonites cancelled his promise to them. Though they had tricked him in the first place and then got him to make a treaty of peace with them, Joshua still felt bound to honor his commitment. So when they called for help, he came to their assistance.

Are you bound to keep a promise based on someone else's lie? It's a tricky moral question, isn't it? But today's story does make us think about integrity—about how we are to practice it in our lives and how we are to keep promises as students, friends, members of a family and also as athletes.

Integrity can be defined as the state of being whole or undivided. That's another way of saying a person who has integrity is honest in following through on his or her commitments to other people, be they parents, coaches, teammates, employers or friends—or even people you may dislike. It means doing what we promised to do, come what may. It means taking seriously that God is our audience of one, even when no one else is there to watch us.

A lack of integrity, on the other hand, leads us to take shortcuts. It means breaking promises, spoken or unspoken, that we made to parents, teachers, coaches or anyone else, including our Lord. It could involve cheating on homework, not working hard in practice when the coach isn't looking, kicking a golf ball out of a bad lie in a tight match, coming in late at night after you promised to be back on time, lying to get out of a tight spot, accepting too much change from a cashier or undercutting a teammate. The possibilities are infinite.

In summer basketball camps, I tell the kids that integrity means knowing the right thing and doing the right thing, no matter what.

Integrity builds trust in families and schools, but also among teammates. When you keep your word, the Lord smiles and everyone benefits. So do you.

CHALLENGES:

Do you ever catch yourself breaking your word?

If you do break your word, what does it do to you? How do you feel about yourself afterward?

FOLLOWING THROUGH

Joshua 11:15

Athletes know about following through. It's vital when you're a pitcher, a golfer, a tennis player, a shooter in basketball, a hitter in softball, a diver or a javelin thrower, just to name a few. If you don't follow through on your stroke, your swing, your dive or your shot, your effort will be wasted.

Following through when we face life's challenges can be harder, but it's just as vital. Joshua is a prime example of someone who didn't quit halfway. He obeyed God's command to rid the land of sin so God's people could occupy it. It took seven years, but he didn't falter. He's an example for all of us.

It can be relatively easy to start most tasks but tougher to complete them. "The road to hell is paved with good intentions," the old saying goes. It is one thing to start something and mean well; it is another to persevere, to follow through when obstacles or distractions mount.

That's true of our intentions as Christians, too, isn't it? We so often fail to follow our Lord all the way. But God asks us to push through in our obedience to Him and in the tasks we face in His name.

When leaders fail to follow through on their commitments, everyone suffers. That's true in athletics, too. It's just as frustrating, however, when those same leaders (team captains, for example) delegate responsibility, only to find out there was no follow-through on the part of teammates to finish the job.

It's easy to become distracted instead of completing the task we've been assigned. So many things threaten to block our way.

But we all know that a chain is no stronger than its weakest link. People who don't follow through are weak links.

Sometimes it's other people who stand in the way of our following through. Maybe we have to delete their numbers from our cell phones and join in with people who will encourage our sense of responsibility. Maybe it's other kinds of distractions that cause us to lose our focus. I'm sure you can name quite a few. Maybe it's making more commitments than we can handle.

Whatever the cause, it's important to follow Joshua's lead and follow through, for Christ's sake—and so that our own deep-down joy may be full.

CHALLENGES:

How does follow-through play a role in your athletic skill?

Why is it harder to work on following through on promises or your tasks than when you're pitching or working on your tennis stroke?

Is it hard for you to follow through on your obligations to God and other people? If it is, what things get in your way?

What do you need to follow through with today?

CARRY ON

Joshua 11:15

Have you ever thought about why your school has trophy cases or why it perhaps displays championship banners on the walls of your gym? It's about tradition, isn't it? It's about reminding fans and players of what your school's teams accomplished in the past, thus encouraging you to follow suit. It's about carrying on the traditions others have developed before you came on the scene.

Joshua's situation was somewhat similar. Moses, his predecessor, had established a tradition of following God's commands. We're told that he "left nothing undone of all that the Lord commanded him." He started the job, took it to a certain time and place, and then passed it on to Joshua for completion.

Joshua, for his part, didn't fret about who would get the credit or crab about the mistakes his predecessor might have made. He humbly carried on what was entrusted to him. He built on the tradition of obedience Moses had faithfully established.

To carry on solid traditions is a good thing. It means that you are building on what others have placed in your hands. You, in turn, can enrich that tradition and then pass it on to those who follow you, whether in your church, your city, your school or your sport. If you plan to go to college, think about carrying on what your family and church have entrusted to you and go to a college with wholesome, Christ-centered traditions, and you most likely will not go wrong.

Carrying on can be a long-term project in athletics, too, but sometimes it requires immediate, specific action. Let me give an example. Once, in a tight away basketball game, with 20 seconds left, our team led by one point, and our opponent had the ball. Three of the five players I put into the defensive lineup were not starters.

Yet I knew they would carry on what their teammates who were starters had begun. They were not in a situation promising them personal glory, but they carried on—and incidentally, we stopped our opponents from scoring and won the game.

It all comes down to being faithful and not putting ourselves first, in our devotion to Christ above all, but also in all we do. Jesus was faithful to the end, and for our everlasting joy and benefit. And we're called to be like Him. To carry on in faith and hope.

CHALLENGES:

What's easier for you: to start a job and see it through or to pick up where someone else has left off?

What athletic tradition do you want to carry on?

Do you as a Christian have the courage to reject or try to change bad traditions and start new ones?

WHO WANTS TO
BE PATIENT?

Joshua 11:18

W ere you ever impatient at a fast-food restaurant when the "fast food" promised you in advertising slogans wasn't fast at all? Today's culture of quick lubes, fast food, high-speed Internet and performance-enhancing drugs leads us to expect speed. We want personal improvement or service *now* and don't want to wait. That's why Jimmy John's presently advertises "Subs so fast you'll freak."

Sometimes we want speed for the sake of efficiency, forgetting that it can also lead to frazzled nerves. Sometimes speed seems to have entertainment or thrill value, as when Germans drive 150 miles per hour on their Autobahn, even for short distances, or when teenagers flout speed limits for the sake of the "high" it gives them.

Speed can be hazardous in more than one sense. Present-day athletes using drugs like steroids for quickly improving strength or speed do so in the knowledge that they are damaging their own bodies. And if they get caught, like the Olympic sprinter Marion Jones or the Yankees' Alex Rodriguez, they also lose respect, if not from their own fans, then surely in the eyes of the general public.

Meaningful change in athletics doesn't happen overnight. It involves hard work for long periods of time. Off-season training using weights or the weight room, conditioning, skill development or pickup games brings results, but not immediately.

How can you keep from becoming discouraged when change takes a long time? For one thing, it's important to look back now and then at the change you have achieved in yourself or have helped bring about in others or your team. When you do so, you'll probably be pleased and inspired to move ahead, but when you're in the middle of it, it's no fun at all. Change takes time, and we want quick results.

It took Joshua and the Israelites seven years to conquer Canaan. They had to stay at it, and it was beastly hard work. No fast success for them.

Change in our spiritual lives usually comes slowly, too. Sin was a problem for even the Apostle Paul, who lamented that despite his stunning conversion, he too easily did the evil he didn't want to do and too often neglected the good he was called to do. Developing a right relationship to God is a lifelong process involving patience and struggle. But be at peace; He is working in us, using His own timetable.

Waiting and patience will pay off, whether in our walk with God or athletics. Working and waiting combined. And there's no quick way of speeding up the process.

CHALLENGES:

Do you ever get discouraged when working at your sport?

Are you ever tempted to take shortcuts?

Do you ever feel a holy impatience when it comes to examining your own spiritual growth?

JOSHUA'S WIN STREAK

Joshua 12:7-24

Have you ever beaten Joshua's win streak? Did you or your team ever win 31 games, races or matches in a row? Joshua and the Israelite army did. After learning their lesson at Ai, they achieved 31 victories without stumbling. Maybe the names of the defeated kings are impossible to pronounce, but you sure can count them. They add up to 31.

The Bible doesn't use the word "teamwork" in describing those wins, but Joshua's army must have worked together smoothly to defeat all those enemies. They clearly had a common focus, a common purpose and a common Lord. Put those together with Joshua's ability at strategy, and you have teamwork and a winning combination, even though they were often underdogs with a smaller army.

It's like that in sports. An effective soccer team won't win simply because it's two deep at every position or because every player is in great shape. Their personal skill level may be wonderful, and they may have plenty of speed and outstanding ball control. But if they don't show teamwork and sharp passing, all those good qualities will be wasted. They'll get in one another's way, won't have many scoring opportunities, will start to yell at one another and will have an individualistic, leaky defense. You can't do it without teamwork.

Teamwork involves everyone: coaches, captains, starters and substitutes. It requires unity, selflessness, caring for others, the proper playing of roles, awareness of a common purpose, focus and discipline. The best coach in the world can't engineer it by himself or herself. Everyone has to participate, both at practice and in games, in order to develop teamwork.

You probably read the sports pages. If you do, you've noticed how sports writers call a team that functions that way a "well-oiled machine." I like the Apostle Paul's analogy in 1 Corinthians 12 better. In that chapter he talks about the various members of the body of Christ, some of whom function as the foot, for example, and others as the eye, the ear or the head. They all have to respect one another, work together and show teamwork if the team, the body, is to function as God intended.

Athletic teams and athletes have to operate that way, too—Christian athletes above all.

CHALLENGES:

What are some of the things that can get in the way of teamwork?

Why is teamwork not only more effective but also more fun?

What can leaders, team members and you do to promote teamwork?

STRENGTHS AND WEAKNESSES

Joshua 13:1

W hat would you do if you jumped into a lake or pool, not realizing it was shallow, broke your spinal cord, became paralyzed from the neck down and had to spend the rest of your life in a wheelchair?

Joni Eareckson Tada had precisely that kind of accident some 26 years ago and since that time has been in a wheelchair, unable to use even her hands. After an intense inner-faith struggle, however, she learned to capitalize on what she still *could* do, not on what she had lost. Today she is an internationally known mouth artist, a talented vocalist, a radio host, an author of 17 books and an advocate for disabled persons worldwide. She clearly has focused on what she still can do.

In today's reading we are told that Joshua had become very old, but it is clear that despite the obstacles old age brings, he still was used by the Lord. Maybe he could no longer physically lead troops into battle, but he could contribute. He was able to set up cities of refuge, help in determining which towns were to be homes for the Levites and speak a critically important farewell message to his people. He, too, was called to use the abilities he still had.

In athletics, unfortunately, the temptation is to focus not on what an individual can do well but on what she or he does not do well. When athletes don't perform at a high level in all phases of the game, fans tend to walk away, shaking their heads—or worse.

But on a team, win or lose, everyone is important, everyone has something to contribute. In softball, perhaps a hitter doesn't have great home run power but excels at bunting or running the bases. In cross country a runner may not have the ability to be first on the team, but in running fifth, he or she can tighten the pack and help make the team successful. In lacrosse, a player may not be talented enough to earn playing time but can be a great help because of his or her leadership and knowledge of the game. Look for those strengths, and use them.

It's important to encourage players with *limited* abilities to do the best with what they have. It not only builds team spirit, it also is an encouragement for the player involved.

God used aged Joshua's wisdom and remaining vitality for the good of the whole nation, even when his physical strength had lessened. That's a lesson for us, too: to emphasize what we can do and to use the strengths God has given us.

CHALLENGES:

Are you able to keep your self-esteem based on what you can do, while working to improve your weaknesses?

Are you an encourager?

What overlooked strengths of your teammates can you encourage?

UNCONQUERED LANDS

Joshua 13:1

You probably heard about him in history class. Alexander the Great, who ruled in the fourth century BC, was an enormously successful king of Macedonia and a fabled military genius. In fact, by the time of his early death he had subdued most of the then-known world. It is said that because he was undefeated in battle, he became depressed early in his 20s, since there were no new lands to conquer.

Most of us don't have that problem. There are plenty of battles yet to be won and lands to conquer. Sometimes there seems to be too many of them. We may have weaknesses in our athletic skills, academic work and our ability to build relationships—or in our decision making when it comes to college choices, career decisions and all the rest. Alexander's lament probably never will be ours. There's plenty of unconquered territory out there.

The Israelites in their conquest of the Promised Land didn't have that problem, either. Today's text tells us in blunt fashion that, as Joshua aged, there were still many "very large areas of land" to be taken over. It was God's will that the conquest be completed. And most importantly, He had repeatedly promised the Israelites that He would be with them and would support them if they kept covenant with Him.

Whatever our age, the size of those unconquered lands can be depressing. We wonder how we will ever make it through and declare our battles won. We wonder about those weaknesses that seem to plague us on so many fronts. At those times we're called to remember the promises God made to Israel and also to us. We will never be struggling alone if we rely on Him and ask for His help.

And there are benefits from the struggle. In them we get to experience our Lord's power and wisdom in new ways. In addition, our battles will enable us to stretch and develop and to learn new things about ourselves and people around us. And they can, if we listen carefully, enable us to practice greater reliance on Him as our king, undefeated in battle.

Whatever lands are left for you to conquer, please remember that your Lord is at your side. And as we are told in Romans 8, "In all these things we are *more than conquerors* through Him who loved us." That's something even Alexander the Great couldn't say.

CHALLENGES:

Which lands do you still have to conquer? Which battles are you facing?

Do you have any friends you need to quietly remind in their struggles that "God is for us"?

LEADING BY SERVING

Joshua 13:14 and 33, 14:3-4

Professional athletes can be quick to protest when they think they've been given a raw deal. Maybe it's a lack of playing time. Maybe it's being traded when they desperately want to stay with a certain team. Who knows? Raw deals come in many shapes.

Did the tribe of Levi get a raw deal when it, unlike the other tribes, wasn't given a chunk of land as its inheritance? Sure, it got grazing rights for its sheep and was given towns that were scattered about, but it did not receive land. Should the Levites have put their foot down and demanded land, come what may?

Well, they didn't. Why not?

In Numbers 8 we learn that the Levites had long since been set apart. They were Israelites "wholly given" to the Lord. They were to perform sacrifices on behalf of the people, sacrifices of atonement, for example.

This special function made the Levites religious leaders. The Israelites came to them with their offerings, but only the Levites could make sacrifices for them. So the broader community needed those Levites. Their service, in a sense, went both ways: They served God and others.

We live in New Testament times and can go directly to our Lord, who became the sacrifice for us. But we still can learn from the role of the Levites, for they suggest that leadership is primarily intended as service.

Leadership is not an opportunity to boss others around, but to serve them. Nobody likes bossy leaders, whether on athletic teams or anywhere else. Jesus didn't come into our world to be a boss, but to be the servant of many. And He calls us to imitate Him.

How do we do that? By not putting ourselves first, but by investing ourselves in the lives of others. Christ Himself tells us that when we care for others, and especially the needy, we are caring for Him. That's awesome, isn't it?

On the court or on the field we can serve others, too—in any number of ways. For starters, you can serve them by encouraging them, by drawing loners into the group, by listening when they're burdened by cares and worries, by calming them down when their temper flares, sometimes even by withholding comment when they already know they've messed up and simply want to move forward.

Service has many faces.

CHALLENGES:

How can you serve your team?

Do you know any real servant leaders? How do they show it?

Is there a needy person close by who needs you? Are you willing to give of yourself to that person?

100 PERCENT BUY-IN

Joshua 14:5

What would it be like if you were suddenly given or bought shares in Nike or Adidas? If that happened, you'd probably follow the financial news more carefully than you do now. You would be a part owner; you would have bought into the company.

If you had no such stock, you'd probably skip that information. Who cares? The sports scores are a lot more interesting than stock market reports.

What does it mean to have stock in something, to "buy in"? To take ownership? To invest? Today's text gives us a partial example. Under Joshua's leadership, the Israelites "divided the land, just as the Lord had commanded Moses." At that moment they totally bought into the Lord's plan and followed it exactly. They made it their own. Joshua, of course, had done so all along.

Unfortunately, at times in their history, the Israelites opted out and sold their stock. They sold it cheap! They wanted out of God's plan, His guidelines and commandments, as they violated His law. The results were always disastrous.

On the other hand, when they bought into His Kingdom plan, the land thrived.

It's something like that in athletics. Buying in means that you give 100 percent to the team, your teammates and your coach. Whether in swimming, football, golf, baseball or any other sport, you adopt the team's goals and make them your own. It's your outfit, and you want it to thrive. You watch its progress carefully and do all you can to help that progress along.

In other words, you take ownership. You respectfully suggest changes when they should be made, of course, and at the right time. You do that because you care. But you're not almost committed or committed some of the time or only when you agree. You're fully committed all of the time.

It's been my experience as a coach that if all team members buy in to the same mission and purpose, the dividends are rich. The season is much more enjoyable and successful. Buying in gives that kind of result.

Buying in to our Lord's goals, with His Spirit leading us, is, of course, the greatest investment of all. Its dividends will be beyond our wildest dreams. Buy into those goals, and you'll see for yourself.

CHALLENGES:

How can you encourage "buy-in" by your teammates?

Have you totally bought into your team's goals and strategies?

What challenges do you face in regard to buy-in in athletics, academics and faith development?

What are some distractions that keep you from buying into the Lord's goals?

FAITHFULNESS AND FINISHING STRONG

Joshua 14:6-15

Examples of faithfulness don't make it into the news very often, it seems, unless they have to do with dogs that in their faithfulness rescue a master or a small child. Human *un*faithfulness seems to be far more newsworthy, especially when it involves the private lives of professional athletes, like ace pitcher Roger Clemens and Tiger Woods.

Today's reading is a wonderful example of the opposite trait, of faith*fulness*. Caleb, as you may remember, was one of the two spies who had scouted out the Promised Land more than 40 years ago and then reported that the country could be conquered, even as the Lord had promised. In doing so, he bucked majority opinion and the fearfulness of his countrymen.

Since that time he had remained faithful to the Lord, and then asked Joshua for the land Moses had promised him those many years ago. He hadn't been faithful just now and then; we read in verse 14 that he had followed the Lord *wholeheartedly*.

It's not always easy to be faithful. Sometimes the price is high, as when Christians under persecution even today remain true to their faith and their Lord. Sometimes remaining faithful can cost you more than friendships; sometimes it can cost your life.

Being faithful is being faith-filled, and being faith-filled is more than attending church, going through the motions and doing what your parents ask. Being faith-filled is a personal matter and requires prayer, self-discipline and wholehearted commitment.

It's a matter of sticking with your Lord, come what may. It's a matter of putting Him first in whatever you do.

Being faithful to Christ not only shapes our spiritual life, it is a model for all we do or think. In athletics, faithfulness means staying true to your team's goals from beginning to end, staying committed to self-discipline, to hard work, to the system, to your teammates—from start to finish, even when your team is in a slump or when it suffers a tough loss.

The Apostle Paul had seen plenty of highs and lows while running his race on behalf of his Lord. But when he was about to break the tape toward the end of his life, he could say, "I have finished the course; I have kept the faith." He did so despite opposition, hardship, beatings, imprisonment and all the rest. That's *real* faithfulness!

CHALLENGES:

Why do you think faithfulness is so important in everyday living?

Why is faithfulness vital to successful athletic teams and programs?

BREAKING IT DOWN

Joshua 14:15b: "Then the land had rest from war."

After seven years of battle Joshua dismissed the army, which then broke down into the 12 tribes that had made up his larger fighting unit. Now it became the responsibility of each of these 12 units to occupy the land assigned to them and to clear out the few enemies that remained. They had worked together for a long time, and each unit had played its role as a member of the team, but now it was time to act individually, by tribe.

In athletics, it's obvious that the team has to function as a unit. But that doesn't cancel out each team member's individuality. Each of us has our own personality, our own weaknesses, our own strengths—and our own responsibilities, too. That's especially true in team sports. One weak link and the chain snaps.

So each individual in a team counts. But working together as a team doesn't mean you have to be the kind of people who think alike on everything, laugh at the same jokes and listen to the same music.

Individual personalities bring wonderful variety into any group. A group that tries to squash individuals creates a drab, colorless monster in which everyone thinks the same. In politics that results in brainwashing and dictatorships, where differences are not allowed.

It's different in the Bible. The Apostle Paul talked about the necessity of teamwork, of everyone working together to form the body of Christ. So it's a practical matter: Without effective individuals a team will be incomplete and will break down. We need one another; each individual is important.

But there's more to it. He also reminds us that those individuals, simply by being themselves, can bring special gifts that benefit everyone. For example, in athletics the enthusiasm of one person can be catching; that may be his or her special contribution. The same is true of a teammate's dedication to conditioning or her or his unique sense of humor.

It's a matter of balance, isn't it? The team depends on teamwork if its effort is to pay off. But that same team is made up of individuals, each of whom counts, including substitutes, and may have something special to contribute. Not so that they make big headlines, but so that the job gets done in a much more diverse and satisfying way.

CHALLENGES:

What have you seen on teams you've been on—too much group thinking and acting or too much individuality, as when one or two people stand out?

Has your team ever been enriched by having unique personalities, "real characters" on it? Think of examples.

What individual responsibilities are you taking on to develop your faith?

PROMISES, PROMISES

Genesis 48:21-22

Joshua 16:4, 21:43-45

Many of us have gotten pretty cynical about promises. This is especially true in politics. Someone recently went so far as to say, "Years ago, fairy tales all began with 'Once upon a time'; now we know they all begin with 'If I am elected.'" We just don't put much stock in political promises anymore.

Politicians aren't the only culprits in this regard. It's easy to make quick promises and sometimes tough to fulfill them, even for your parents. But broken promises hurt. Haven't you heard small children wail as they say to a parent, "But you promised!" Sometimes it is actually impossible to keep promises, of course, since circumstances change; more often we only *think* we can't keep them. However, promises are not made to be forgotten or broken.

In several of these devotionals we've thought about trust and how important it is in athletics. Trust is built on promises made and kept. When you join a team, you make several promises simply by joining. If you break them, either intentionally or by neglect, you break trust, and with broken trust comes upset, disappointment, a breakdown in team chemistry and failure.

In today's reading we see how a promise the dying Jacob made to Joseph way back in Egypt was actually kept many years later when Joshua allotted Joseph's descendants their promised territory. But we also see something far greater and more assuring when we read that "Not one of the Lord's good promises to the house of Israel failed; every one was fulfilled." *Every single one.* That's a pretty good record of promise keeping.

The writer of Psalms says the same thing in Psalm 145: "The Lord is faithful to all His promises and loving toward all He has made." God is the first promise keeper.

You can make bad promises based on evil intentions, of course, as in "I promise I'll get even." But the Psalmist says the Lord is both faithful *and* loving. As He makes and keeps His promises to all eternity, He is motivated only by love. His example calls us to make thoughtful promises and then, with His help, to keep them—in every area of our lives.

CHALLENGES:

What would be the results if someone tracked the promises you made against those you actually kept?

What are some reasons (or excuses) that can make it hard to keep promises?

What promises have you made—to others, to yourself, to the Lord? What steps are you taking to keep them?

RUNNING STEEP HILLS

Joshua 16:10

I f you're a cross country runner, you know all about running up steep hills. It's rough. It can make your lungs burn, your side ache and your legs grow weak, if you haven't trained properly. Maybe you're tempted to quit halfway up. You're tired of it all.

As we've already noted, that seems to be what happened to the Israelites. Perhaps out of sheer weariness they failed to drive out the pagan Canaanites, as the Lord had commanded them. They wanted to settle down *now* and didn't think about the future results of allowing the Canaanites to continue living where they were. Who cares about tomorrow? Perhaps this last hill of ridding the land of them seemed just too steep to climb. They thought they knew what was best for them right now.

It can be hard to look ahead and not get caught in the present. That's surely true of our lives before the Lord. It's easier to forget our faith commitment now and then, to get in the habit of telling white lies, of cheating in schoolwork, of skipping personal devotions when we're tired, of failing to help a hurting classmate or of cultivating unhealthy relationships, for example. We don't want to think about future consequences of today's actions for ourselves or for others. It's easier to live our lives by what feels good today.

That's true in athletics, too. It's sometimes tempting to go halfway in preseason conditioning or to slack off in wind sprints, to judge that you've done enough for now and be satisfied. But as the season nears its end, you'll face some tough hills in the form of close games with five minutes to go, for example, when you need all the strength and stamina you can muster. Poor conditioning will produce disastrous results in such situations.

On the other hand, thinking ahead and preparing in advance, though it may be unpleasant, will pay off in stressful, demanding situations in the future. Any coach will tell you that.

Developing good habits of honesty, faithfulness and commitment as young Christians will surely help give us strength when we hit tomorrow's hills. It's important to live today to the fullest, but it's just as important to remember our tomorrows, for our own sake, for the sake of others and for the sake of our Lord.

CHALLENGES:

Do you usually think ahead?

Is it hard for you as a busy young Christian to "keep your eyes on [the Lord's] prize"?

What can you do today to help you prepare for the future?

HALF-COURT TO FULL-COURT—HANDLING CHANGE

Joshua 17:3-6

You've probably heard your grandparents talk about how things have changed since their childhood. Back then there were no computers, no cell phones, no iPods, no TVs, no helicopters, no jet planes, no microwave ovens and all the rest.

Athletics have changed, too. Women's basketball is radically different from what it was in the 1940s or early '50s, when half of the team stayed behind the center line and played defense, while offensive team members stayed on the other half of the court. And men's basketball has changed from a guard-but-don't-touch game to a modified contact sport.

Today's reading from Joshua shows change, too. As the land was being divided, it was the sons who inherited their assigned area. Daughters were scarcely mentioned in the process. Israelite society was in many ways male-oriented. But here we had five daughters who showed up and claimed their father's inheritance, since there were no sons in the family. The Israelite males must have raised their eyebrows and scratched their heads. This surely was a change in the way things were done.

As you move from one level of your sport to the next, you surely will experience change as well, as you get different coaches, each of whom does things just a bit differently. And all of them have different personalities and different expectations. If you go on to play in college, the change will be even more noticeable.

What's the key to managing change so that you benefit and your coaches can coach you effectively?

What's true in sports is true in the rest of life, too. You have to be willing to accept change and lead yourself and your team effectively through it. In this way, all can benefit from it. You have to learn what to keep and what to throw away. Adapt, but never throw away the essentials.

It's surely that way in your life as a young Christian, too. As you grow older, you'll become more aware of what remains vital to a life lived for your Lord and what childhood practices you have now outgrown.

The comforting thing in this sometimes confusing process is the fact that the Lord is "the same yesterday, today and forever." And if you ask Him, He'll guide you through every change you'll have to make. Every single one.

CHALLENGES:

Do you find it difficult to adjust to change at home, in school, in athletics?

Do you get impatient when others around you won't change?

What is most comforting in knowing that God doesn't change? How does knowing that help you?

Consider this thought: Either you get better or worse; you never stay the same.

JUST DO IT

Joshua 17:14-18

Excuses can be funny. Police officers, principal's offices and especially insurance companies have a big stock of them, like excuses for damaging a car: "Coming home, I drove into the wrong driveway and hit a tree I don't have" or "The telephone pole was approaching fast. I was attempting to swerve out of its path when it struck my front end."

Our everyday excuses are less creative. "I was going to do it, but I forgot." "I didn't know it had to be done today." "My printer crashed before I could type up my paper." "I didn't have time." "It's just too boring." "My friends were waiting for me." "It was way too hard for me."

In today's reading, the people of Joseph (the tribes of Ephraim and Manasseh) thought they had good excuses for not claiming the land assigned them. They first said the cleared space in their assigned territory was too small, then added that the Canaanites who lived there had iron chariots. Joshua was unimpressed, telling them to clear the forested area and drive out the enemy. In short, he told them to quit making excuses and get to it.

Athletes can be good at excuses, too. A friend of mine once knew of an 800-meter runner who frequently faked a pulled muscle when he saw he was going to lose a race. (That's a "lame" excuse, if ever there was one.) Other excuses can include "I'm not tall enough, quick enough, strong enough, and my teammates didn't pass me the ball enough." Or "Why go all out, when my coach scarcely notices me?" When we behave that way, we're not claiming the gifts God gave us and making the most of them. Steve Prefontaine, once America's premier middle- and long-distance runner, put it this way: "To do less than your best is to waste the gift."

Sometimes we have to just stop the excuses and get the work done.

That's true in our spiritual lives, too. It's easy to find excuses for not doing our devotions, for skipping church, for ignoring needy friends, for fighting with a brother or sister ("He/she started it"), for generally cutting corners when the Lord asks obedience of us. Perhaps the worst excuse of all is one we've heard too often: "I'm not perfect, you know."

When you're tempted to make excuses for not doing the right thing, pray to the Lord who never used them. He's certainly more pleased with even your fumbling attempts at obedience than He is with your excuses. He can give you the strength to "just do it." Why wait?

CHALLENGES:

What kind of excuses do you find yourself using for a task poorly done or not done at all?

How do teammates who constantly make excuses affect team morale?

How do you lead despite the excuses teammates may make?

TOMORROW, MAYBE

Joshua 18:1-6

"Tomorrow," "later" and "sometime" are three of the more popular words in the vocabulary of many of us. "I'll clean my room tomorrow," "I'll do my homework later" (that probably should be first on the list), "I'll write thank you notes for my birthday gifts when I have more time." Or if you're a high school senior, "I'll apply for college admission when I get around to it."

Why do we put things off? Is it because the task seems too boring, too tough, too unpleasant? Is it fear that we'll fail? Or do we think that some projects will just go away, if we forget about them? We know better, of course, but procrastination is a tendency that is as old as the human race.

It's surely as old as the people of Israel. In today's Scripture reading Joshua scolded the seven remaining tribes for their failure to take the land the Lord has given them. You can hear the impatience in his words just as clearly as you can when your parents are exasperated when you haven't done what has to be done *now*. Joshua was clearly asking why he had to push those seven tribes to do something they already knew they ought to do.

Shoving problems or necessary tasks aside will probably make them worse. For example, if you delay discussing a difficult issue with parents, a friend, a coach or a teacher, your own tension or fear will increase. And the situation won't improve.

As a coach, I have an open door for my players. I invite them to come to discuss any problems or concerns they may have. Some do; some don't. One thing I know: Communication is better than procrastination. Open talk can heal many situations before they get worse.

Spiritual procrastination hurts, too. Maybe it's making a public profession of our faith that gets put off. Maybe it's mending a broken relationship with a brother or sister or with someone on the team—or even your coach. Delaying acts of obedience to our Lord in our everyday lives can so easily become a habit that finally destroys our peace and joy.

But once again, to pray to the Lord who promises us strength for *this* day is to take a long step in the right direction. And don't wait until "tomorrow, maybe" to pray that prayer. Do it today. You'll be glad you did.

CHALLENGES:

Have you ever put something off and found the consequences to be much worse because of your delay?

Do you have anything you're putting off that you should be taking care of now?

What steps should you be taking to get at it?

NICE GUYS FINISH LAST?

Joshua 19:49-50

Have you ever heard the quote "Nice guys finish last"? A famous baseball manager, Leo Durocher, made that claim way back in 1939.

Ty Cobb was a baseball player, arguably the greatest player of all time, who lived and played that way. No finishing last for him. His lifetime batting average was .366, and he set 100 major league records during his career. But in his dealings both on and off the field he was known to be surly, aggressive and totally unlikeable. One sports writer described his playing style as "ferocious." Ty Cobb was not a nice guy, and he surely *never* finished last.

On the other hand, when it came to parceling out land for the 12 tribes, Joshua, the acknowledged leader of all Israel, was a prime example of a good person who gracefully finished last. Only after each of the tribes had been allotted their land did he receive his share. He waited until everyone else was served before claiming what was his.

Anyone who wants to be a leader on her or his team could well take Joshua as an example. He was a servant leader in the New Testament tradition: not a person who put himself first, but one who was more interested in the good of others.

Servant leaders won't tolerate hazing, either. It's a destructive practice that runs counter to what it means to be a Christian athlete. If your coach has chosen you to be on the team, that's enough. You don't have to undergo humiliation to be accepted.

Your acceptance has already happened.

In a sense, Joshua was like Jesus Himself. Our Lord, shaper of the universe and undisputed leader of the Christian church to all eternity, had every right to put Himself first. But He most surely considered the needs of His people first, even though it took Him to a grisly cross.

As we've noted before, churches, governments, financial leaders and athletic teams need leaders like that. And not just leaders. All of us are called to live that way.

You've no doubt heard the well-worn saying that it's "God first, others second and you last." You may be tired of hearing it, but that's what the Christian life is all about. And in the final judgment, good people, saved by God's grace, will not come in last. Our Lord measures winning differently from the way the world does today. Praise be to Him alone!

CHALLENGES:

What could putting others first mean for your team?

What characteristics of Christ will it take to be a servant leader?

STORM SHELTERS

Joshua 20:1-6

Tornadoes and hurricanes have been very much in the news. As I write this devotional, people are commemorating the fifth anniversary of Hurricane Katrina, which tore up large parts of the Gulf Coast, including New Orleans. When such storms develop, whether in our country or abroad, people are immediately urged to seek shelter, to find a place of refuge to escape the devastation.

There's another kind of devastation as well, one resulting not from storms in nature, but from accidents that kill. Not only can such a tragedy cripple or destroy the life of the victim, it can also cause terrible guilt feelings in the person responsible for the accident, even when it was unintentional. In the Old Testament, in addition to bearing feelings of guilt, the person who caused death without intending to do so rightly feared that he could be pursued and killed by an avenger. For instances like these the Lord provided cities of refuge to which such a person in flight could go and get a fair trial.

Fortunately, few of us have driven cars that plowed into trees or another vehicle, costing the life of our passenger and leaving us with deep guilt. Maybe we aren't threatened by tornadoes or hurricanes, either, but life itself can sometimes become stormy. Broken relationships, unfair treatment by a teacher or coach, the divorce of parents, being forced to move to a different town and school, the death of a parent, being benched, going through a long losing streak—all of them can cause furious storms. Where can we find our cities of refuge?

Many people can help provide us with a safe haven. Parents, sisters or brothers can be such safe places, helping us weather our storms. Church can be that kind of place. Friends, teachers and coaches can provide refuge. We all know, however, that the ultimate place of refuge is in the Lord. As the old hymn puts it, Jesus is "a shelter in the time of storm."

Where can we find Him? The Bible with its many promises is a wonderfully safe refuge where He speaks words of comfort and hope. Pouring out our struggles in prayer is yet another place where we can meet Him, if we pray with faith and an open heart. Mature Christians can also be of great help in our search for Him, if we listen to them.

That may not mean that the storms are stilled immediately. But His promises don't fail. Thus the old proverb, "God promises a safe landing, but not a calm passage." Never forget the safe landing. Your storms will never have the last word.

CHALLENGES:

Are you going through a particularly rough storm right now?

Do you remember making it safely through past storms?

Are you willing to be a city of refuge for teammates going through storms?

ALL BY YOURSELF?

Joshua 21:43-45

The century now past gave voice to some pretty hefty boasts. Mohammed Ali was the greatest boxer of his time, but the boast he made was pretty comprehensive: "I'm the greatest," he said over and over. The greatest. Not just the greatest boxer. Then there was Winston Churchill, who led England victoriously through World War II and the Nazi menace. When challenged at one point while writing his memoirs, he responded with the line, "But I'm a great man." It's almost funny, isn't it?

Joshua had clearer vision in such matters. Nowhere in the chapters of Joshua we've considered do we read that Joshua boasted after the Israelite army had subdued its foes. As the texts in today's reading indicate, it was the Lord who had won the battles, and Joshua knew it. To claim the glory for himself or his army would have been a great offense to his Lord.

Boasting is dumb, stupid, isn't it? In the first place, if you're really that great, you won't have to blow your own horn. Second, by boasting you show your own weakness, as you try to build yourself up in the eyes of others. Third, boasting is one of the quickest ways to lose friends and the respect of people around you.

And most importantly, any abilities we have in academics or sports or any other areas are gifts from God. As Eric Liddell, the British 400-meter champion in the '24 Olympics, put it in the movie *Chariots of Fire*, "God made me fast." A nearly 200-year-old hymn expresses that thought differently; its first line is "All that I am I owe to Thee." All of it. You never do it alone.

You're not alone in your sport, either. Any goal you score in soccer or hockey was set up by one or two teammates, maybe more. Any basket you make is preceded by a good pass, a screen someone set for you, or someone's cutting to vacate an area for you. And if you set a triple jump record, you've done so because of the coaching and encouragement of others.

Ultimately, however, whatever you accomplish is the result of God's good gifts. Healthy pride acknowledges that fact. Realizing it will bring the Lord the credit due Him and will only increase your own grateful joy.

CHALLENGES:

Are there ways of quiet boasting without saying anything out loud? Think about it.

How can boasting affect team morale and unity?

JUST HELP

Joshua 22:4

A friend of mine was once at an Amish worship service. At its beginning, one of the very oldest members of the community stood up and began to read aloud the Scripture for the day. The Bible he read was very old, very large, and very heavy. It was no surprise when his hands began to shake, first just slightly, then more and more severely.

A young man in his early 20s then got up from his bench and walked to the aged reader, but not to take his place, not to finish reading the passage for him. Instead, he stood in front of him and placed his hands beneath the trembling hands of the older man, steadying them, and thus enabling him to finish his reading.

That's the kind of help the Reubenites, Gadites, and half-tribe of Manasseh had given, as today's passage indicates. They had gone in to help the other tribes conquer their share of Canaan, and then were given permission to withdraw. They asked nothing for their services and did not demand recognition for what they had accomplished. They had simply enabled the other tribes to take over their inheritance and begin serving the God who had redeemed them. And that was enough.

We have many, many opportunities to help others live meaningful and blessed lives. Perhaps it is a mission trip in which we prayerfully provide finances and actual physical help to build orphanages or church buildings, so that the orphanage or church can do what it is called to do. Closer to home, perhaps it's doing odd jobs for an aged neighbor so that she or he can continue to live at home. Maybe it's befriending a new kid in class and helping him fit in and move forward. The possibilities are endless.

As team members, we can encourage fellow players who are struggling and thus enable them to reach their potential. Sometimes just listening to a troubled team member is a wonderful way to help. Holding another player responsible is yet another way of helping him or her to progress. Frequently the help we give will be quiet and done in private. But a public act, like helping a teammate or even an opponent off the floor, can also help the spiritual development of younger fans who are watching.

Whatever the form of the help we give, God must surely smile as He sees it. And who could want more?

CHALLENGES:

Are you ignoring anyone in your life who clearly needs your help?

Do you find it hard to accept help? If you find it difficult, why?

How can letting others help you be a blessing to them?

FACT AND FICTION

Joshua 22:9-34

What happened in today's reading? The tribes of Israel were prepared to engage in civil war against the Gadites, the Reubenites and the half-tribe of Manasseh because they assumed, or heard rumor, that they were building an imposing altar to pagan gods and thus violating God's direct command.

Fortunately, war was headed off because the Israelite tribes took the time to send a delegation to find out what Reuben and Gad's intentions in building that altar really were. Upon asking, the Israelites learned, to their great relief, that this newly built altar was meant to be a holy witness that "the Lord is God." After hearing the truth, the delegation returned home, dismissed the troops and told their thankful people the good news. Our reading tells us that devastation had thus been averted.

The world of athletics, especially on the professional level, is a hotbed of rumor, and thanks to Twitter, blogs and the Internet, they spread like wildfire. It's hard to know what's true and what's not. Often we seem to prefer rumor to truth; it's more fun, more interesting.

For example, current rumor has it that Tiger Woods' wife smacked him over the head with a three iron and that her divorce settlement gave her $650 million. In baseball, today's silly rumor claims that Manny Ramirez won't cut his dreadlocks when he joins the White Sox, despite team policy. In football, current rumor says that quarterback Matt Leinart may be cut from the Arizona Cardinals because his teammates lack faith in him, despite his performance. Other rumors can be far, far more vicious in nature. Who really knows the truth? Do we really care?

Going to the source of the rumor and trying to unearth the truth can be less interesting than listening to and spreading rumors. But we can avoid big trouble if we're willing to do some digging.

Rumors may sometimes be funny, but many times they bring devastation—in the form of broken friendships, ruined reputations, mistrust, heartbreak and more. No, rumors often are not funny at all.

That's surely true with teams. Listening to rumors about a teammate or a coach can cause breakdown on many levels. It's a matter of thinking the best of others and developing healthy communication. We honor one another and our Lord when we take the time to work toward the truth in every part of our lives.

In the book of John, Jesus Himself says that "the truth will set you free." It really will.

CHALLENGES:

Have you ever been hurt by a rumor?

Do you have the courage to step up in front of your friends and put an end to rumors about others?

How can rumors hurt team unity?

SWAN SONGS

Joshua 23, 24:15

W hen I think of farewell speeches—"swan songs," as they are sometimes called—many people come to mind. Some gave talks that were full of anger and bitterness about what had happened in their lives. But surely not all of them. Not in athletics, either.

Take, for example, Ernie Harwell, the baseball Hall of Fame announcer who was the broadcast voice of the Detroit Tigers for 55 years. Ernie closed out his career with, "I praise the Lord here today. I know that all my talent and all my ability come from Him, and without Him, I'm nothing, and I thank Him for His great blessing." Harwell did not focus on himself and his achievements in his swan song, although he was a giant in the world of sports journalism.

Joshua spoke a model swan song, as recorded in chapters 23 and 24. In it he did not remind the Israelites of what he had done, but what the Lord had done. He was straightforward and honest, as he both warned the people of the dire consequences of disobedience and idolatry and reminded them of the Lord's wonderful promises if they love and serve Him alone. He told of the Lord's great faithfulness, and he pleaded with the Israelites to be faithful in return. And he closed it with the pledge that he and his family would serve the Lord.

There's a wonderful line in *The Shack*, a book by William P. Young: "If anything is important, everything is important." Everything. We're called to serve the Lord in all that we do.

Both big and small acts of obedience and love matter to the Lord.

They matter a lot in our lives at home, in school, in church, in our entertainment, in friendships and all the rest. And they matter in athletics.

Among those big acts of obedience and love might be treating your opponents with respect and not making an idol of your sport, for example. Smaller acts might include such things as forgiveness when an opponent roughs you up unnecessarily, thanking your coach for teaching you something new and encouraging a substitute player who has few chances to play.

Loving obedience will bring the Lord's blessing in His good time; though His forgiveness will not fail, disobedience will bring hurt. With Joshua, we're called every morning to "choose whom we will serve." The right choice will make all the difference and will ultimately lead to a swan song of gratitude, praise and grace.

CHALLENGES:

If you were at the end of your career, what would you like to be able to say in your swan song?

Why is it important to make a conscious effort to choose to serve Jesus each day leading up to your swan song?

HOPEFUL REALISM: KNOW YOUR WEAKNESSES

Joshua 23:6-13

I once read a story about a young amateur baseball player in the 1920s. His name was Mike Todd. Could that guy hit! He didn't knock the cover off the ball just now and then; he did so regularly. He soon became an authentic hometown hero, so that when he boarded the bus for his Big League tryout, a large crowd gathered to see him off. If anybody could make it to the top, he could.

A few weeks later, however, the scene was different. He did not come home to a welcoming crowd at the bus station, for the bubble had burst. Maybe he could hit a fastball a mile, but he couldn't touch a curve. Neither he nor his local admirers had realized that weakness. And now he came home with a bruised spirit.

In today's reading, Joshua approached the Israelites quite differently. He knew exactly the potential weaknesses of his people and didn't cheer them on. He knew they would be prone to serve false gods and their idols. He knew they would be tempted to intermingle with the pagans living among them, even to the point of marrying them. He knew the danger of pride in their military achievements. Joshua pulled no punches when it came to identifying weaknesses.

Seeing your own weaknesses in your life as a young Christian can be a big help. It can help you avoid all forms of pride and especially spiritual pride. It can help you withstand temptation, can show you what you need to work on, can help you be humble and gracious, and can give you greater compassion for other people who fight temptation, but stumble and fall anyway.

Recognizing your weaknesses is important in athletics, too, both for you as an individual and for your team. It can assist in developing a game plan, and it can show you what you need to work on and capitalize on, among other things. It can even help you appreciate your strengths and the strengths of your teammates.

Ultimately, recognizing your weaknesses in all of life can lead you to greater dependence on your Lord. And that's always a good thing. As the Apostle Paul writes in 2 Corinthians, "For when I am weak, then I am strong." We can be strong in our total reliance on our Lord, with a strength that will ultimately bring hope, joy and peace.

CHALLENGES:

Do you know your own weaknesses?

How will you work to improve on your weaknesses?

KNOW YOUR STRENGTHS

Joshua 23:8

Yesterday's devotional was about weaknesses. Today's is about strengths.

Playing major league ball for the San Francisco Giants, Tim Lincecom is 5-foot-11 and is currently batting a measly .105. However, Tim's strength is in his pitching, where he has won the Cy Young Award as the best pitcher in the National League for the past two seasons.

Today's reading is about strengths, too. In it Joshua complimented the people of Israel on their past strength and admonished them to build on it for the future. This compliment had nothing to do with their military conquests; it was their proven ability to "hold fast" to the Lord their God that Joshua identified as their strong point. That's the strength he asked them to capitalize on—the most important one of all.

Having prominent strengths can, of course, carry with it a temptation to become proud and arrogant. But recognizing where these abilities originated will promote humility, a smile on your face and a head held high in happy gratitude to God.

Possessing certain strengths in athletics is a great and good gift from the Lord and can be a tremendous asset to any team. If you've got a great three-point shooter, use him or her. If you have an exceptional sprinter, capitalize on it. If you've got a great quarterback, by all means, make the most of it. If you have a fast and accurate striker in soccer, pass to him. And by all means, don't envy them, but cheer these outstanding athletes on.

Utilizing your strengths doesn't mean neglecting your

weaknesses, of course. It's very important to both work on your weaknesses *and* to further develop your strengths.

Each of us is called to use our strengths for His Kingdom, both in athletics and elsewhere.

If playing the trumpet is one of your strengths, play it for the Lord. If your strength is in the sprints, keep running fast. If you're a skilled writer, keep writing. If your strength is leading Bible studies, keep doing it. If you can set records in the butterfly, more power to you. If you're a sensitive teammate, keep listening. And if you're a great encourager, keep encouraging.

Done in gratitude to God, exercising these strengths is one more way of "holding fast" to His goodness and mercies.

CHALLENGES:

Everyone has strengths; what are some of yours?

How can you help your teammates recognize their strengths?

WRONG-WAY CORRIGAN

Joshua 23:16

Did you ever hear of "Wrong-Way Corrigan"? Douglas Corrigan was a pilot back in 1938 who took off from New York with a flight plan indicating Long Beach, California, as his destination, but he went the wrong way and landed instead in Ireland. Further investigation showed that he planned this stunt all along, but the humorous nickname stuck: "Wrong-Way Corrigan."

In the Bible, doing a "Wrong-Way Corrigan" was not at all funny. And the Israelites were good at it. As we noted before, that's why Joshua warned them so strongly against it. God had devised their flight plan, a plan that would lead to peace, joy and hope, and the consequences of going a different way were nasty: His anger would burn against them and they would "quickly perish from the good land [He] had given them."

God was infinitely patient with his Wrong Way Corrigans in the Old Testament. He was "slow to anger, abounding in love," as Psalm 103 puts it. But that love could show itself in His anger and take the form of "tough love," in which the Israelites suffered terribly as a result of their willfulness. They needed somehow to learn that actions had consequences, that sinful choices would eventually bring pain and devastation. Ignoring the flight plan can cost you terribly. Crashes are no fun, even if we survive them.

It's true in athletics, too, isn't it? Athletes who ignore the rules might get their team in deep trouble, and they may get thrown out of the game. In soccer or hockey, that would make for one less player and would jeopardize the team's chance of victory.

The same thing is true of ignoring a game plan and not playing within the system. Not only will it get you benched; it also will break team morale and invite defeat. And defeat is not what you've aimed for.

The Lord most likely won't take you out of the game of life if you ignore His way and stubbornly move out on your own, but the long walk back to His pathway of peace and hope may be rocky, steep and dotted with fearful pitfalls—even though He will forgive you and walk beside you as you struggle to find your way back. But why invite pain and guilt by ignoring His travel instructions in the first place? He wrote them so that you could have a wonderful, fruitful trip and a joyous homecoming.

CHALLENGES:

Have you or a teammate ever cheated or defied training and the rules of your sport? What were the results?

How can you ensure that you walk in the truth?

CHARACTER

Joshua 24:15

D o you think participation in sports develops character? Coaches disagree on the answer to that question. One coach I know says that if you don't have character to begin with, sports won't help you achieve it. Others insist that being an athlete helps you learn discipline, a sense of teamwork, selflessness and all the rest. So, do athletics build character or only reveal it?

The term "character" itself is slippery and is used in many different ways. In sports, a team that won't give up is often described as having "real character," even if some of its players are dishonest—or worse—in their personal lives or at school. Furthermore, there are evil people who won't give up, either, and no one would describe them as having character. Perhaps we ought to use that term more carefully.

There's no question about Joshua, however; he definitely was a person with admirable, godly character. He had shown it in a long life of obedience, faithfulness and trust, and he capped it off with the wonderful pledge "… as for me and my household, we will serve the Lord."

Whether you're an athlete or not, there's no better promise you can ever make than that one. It's a promise that is too important to delay—a promise to build your life on.

But it's not a promise for the faint-hearted. Standing up for what you believe takes character, courage—guts, if you will. Refusing to give in to the lure of alcohol or drugs can cost you friends. Trusting your Lord when things go wrong can demand a lot of you. Quietly rebuking a friend or acquaintance for profanity takes strength. Bucking racism can make you unpopular. Refusing to cheat in schoolwork can hurt your grade. In short, living out that pledge to serve the Lord isn't always easy; it takes character, real character.

Being an athlete with Christian character also means many things: not taking revenge, supporting fellow players and your coach, treating your opponent generously and not as your enemy, keeping your training promises and much, much more. It's all part of serving the Lord. And there are temptations at every bend in the road.

But you're never walking alone, for He has promised to be with you always, if you ask Him. Always.

CHALLENGES:

Does your participation in athletics reveal character, help you develop it or both? How?

If you promise to serve the Lord, what challenging situations do you foresee?

THAT GIANT STEP

Joshua 24:16-18

The ball was in the Israelites' court. Joshua had just served a strong challenge by saying that he and his family were committed to serve the Lord. Would the Israelites return the ball solidly by saying the same thing, or would they hit it into the net by responding weakly?

They surely talked a good line, didn't they? They not only said they would serve the Lord but they gave their reasons for doing so: He brought us up out of Egypt, He performed great signs, He protected us in our travels, He drove out the nations inhabiting the Promised Land before us, including the Amorites.

In short, what they said was, "We have every reason to serve the Lord and to proclaim that He is our God. How could we serve anyone else? We're not *that* stupid."

But there's a radical difference between "talking the talk" and "walking the walk." Actually doing it is usually much harder than just saying it.

In athletics, we're sometimes close relatives of those Israelites when we talk about commitment, communication, trust, team chemistry and leadership. We tend to make big promises and resolutions, but then we hit the ball into the net over and over again. It's important that we remind ourselves daily that *today* we have to live out that talk, that *today* we actually communicate, trust and commit. *That we just do it.*

That's true in every aspect of our lives, isn't it? It's true in our life of faith, too. A friend of mine who was also a college chaplain was fond of saying that "each day we ought to renew our faith with fervor, as if it were the first day of our conversion." And every day we should take that giant step from talk to obedience.

And remember, Jesus is at your side, helping you take that step over and over again.

CHALLENGES:

What examples have you seen where athletes have "talked the talk" but not "walked the walk"?

Why don't we "just do it" more consistently? What gets in our way?

Is there any one area in your life as a young Christian where you need to stop talking and start doing?

(NOT) GOING GREEN

Joshua 24:19a: "He is a holy God; He is a jealous God."

In today's world there's a lot of talk about going green and what that means. Newspapers and TV clips encourage us to leave cars at home, to ride bikes and to minimize the carbon footprint we leave behind us.

There's one area in our lives in which we don't want to "go green," however.

It's the human tendency to envy, to jealousy—commonly called "the green-eyed monster." It's another form of the self-idolatry that harms our walk with our Lord and the people around us and threatens our own peace and joy.

Where does it come from, and how does envy function in our lives?

Instead of being thankful for what God has given to us personally and to those around us, we see the gifts others show as threats to our own idol of self-image or prestige. In athletics we can become envious of teammates' playing time, the attention they get, their ability to lead, their speed, strength, or scoring, their popularity, their decision-making ability and so on.

In the process we hurt ourselves by showing a negative spirit and dark emotions, and we even damage our God-given sense of self-worth. We also destroy team chemistry and unity; everyone gets hurt.

The Lord God is the only person with a right to envy, to the jealousy emphasized in today's passage. He's up-front about saying He is a jealous God who won't accept any form of idol worship. I wonder whether His jealousy about foreign idols isn't in part because of His great love for us. Idols, including the idol of self, do get in the way of the perfect peace the Bible promises us, after all, the peace that He wants for all of His children.

Today is a good day, with God's help, to start appreciating the gifts He has given others—and the unique gifts He has given you: to throw away the idol of self-centered envy and replace it with a thankful spirit.

It's not an easy idol to get rid of, but everyone, including yourself, will be the better for it.

And your Lord will help you and rejoice with you when He sees that green-eyed monster limping off into the distance.

CHALLENGES:

Is there anyone in your life you're jealous of?

How can envy spoil your peace and your relationship with God?

What steps can you take to replace your jealousy and improve your relationship with God?

FUNDAMENTALS

Joshua 24:14-29

I've been blessed by coaching many games in NCAA tournaments. As is true for the first game of the year, the team that best executes the fundamentals in the tournament will win and will come out on top. It's that simple. It's not primarily about one or two star players; it's all about commitment to team fundamentals and then executing them.

Joshua knew about both fundamentals—and about idols. If it's necessary to throw away our idols, it is just as important to keep the fundamentals God lays out for us, to hang onto them with all our strength.

Those fundamentals stand rock-solid. Worship styles may change, the songs we sing in church may be replaced, mission and evangelistic methods may be revised, preaching characteristics may differ radically from church to church or from culture to culture, but the basic realities of sin and forgiveness must stand steady if the church is to be faithful to its Lord. Those truths are the foundation on which we can build with everlasting hope.

There are certain basic fundamentals in all of life, whether in teaching, building, painting, nursing, accounting or in any other trade or profession—in athletics, too. Ignore the fundamentals in tennis, the shot put, playing the outfield, coaching, tending goal in hockey or defending in soccer, and your effort will fail.

That's true above all in our relationship to our Lord. Ignore the foundation He provides us, and we will run aground. His Word, His promises in Christ, His directions for faithful living are fundamental and an absolutely solid foundation for living all of life victoriously, both in good times and bad.

Build on those fundamentals, and you'll see that they make life worth living.

CHALLENGES:

Do you ever get tired hearing about fundamentals in athletics? Why?

Do you and older Christians ever disagree about what your faith's fundamentals really are and about what finally matters in the Christian life?

If so, how can you try to solve the problem?

ME, AN IDOL?

Joshua 24:23

In earlier devotionals we talked about keeping our commitments to God and others by what we do and say. Today's reading reminds us that we may have to toss out some baggage along the way if we are going to turn our pledges into reality.

Have you ever seen *Hoarders* on the A&E network? It's a TV show that chronicles the life of people who have collected so much stuff that it interferes with their living the way they could and should.

Even if you're not a hoarder or pack rat, however, throwing stuff away can be difficult. Most of the time it is more comfortable to keep the things we've gotten used to than it is to clean house.

On a spiritual level, Joshua understood that all too well. That's why he flat out commanded the Israelites to get rid of the foreign gods among them. They weren't just to hide them in a dark corner of the basement or under the bed. They were to throw them away, for they were a sure hindrance to serving God.

One such idol that is foreign to the Kingdom of God can be self. We can become so obsessed with *our* plans, *our* goals, *our* needs, that we clutter, and even block, the pathway to loving our Lord first, to obeying Him and to loving our neighbor. We let our *selves* become the idols blocking the way to obedience and peace.

In the process, we degrade our Lord into a "come-along Jesus," where we make our plans and expect Him to follow us, instead of following the way He has laid out for us in His wisdom and love. And we do it despite Jesus' clear statement, "*I am the way and the truth and the life.*"

It's hard, just plain hard, to throw out that idol of self that wants to set its own course and walk down its own road, expecting Jesus to tag along. It's an idol made of tough stuff. But to allow it to subtly rule our lives is to put things upside-down. And we won't make progress in following the Lord when we're standing on our heads.

When a local high school soccer coach recently retired, he said it had been his joy to help athletes become fully involved in something bigger than themselves—the team. That is a wonderful blessing that can come from participating in team sports.

Every one of us is involved in a Kingdom infinitely greater than ourselves. And by God's grace, it's vital to work at throwing out the idol of self, if ever we're going to enjoy citizenship in that Kingdom—and finally make it home.

CHALLENGES:

Do you seek God's will for your life before making your own plans?

How can you learn what His will is? Do you need others to help you?

A STONE ON
YOUR DRESSER?

Joshua 24:14-27

In the first part of today's passage we saw how Joshua almost goaded the Israelites toward a pledge of faithful service to their Lord. Twice they responded with a promise that they would, in fact, remain faithful.

But Joshua wasn't quite satisfied with their promises. First he declared that Israel was witness against itself that it had made these strong pledges. They had heard what they themselves had said, and their own words would stand to condemn them if they fell short.

And then, to strengthen the idea of witness, Joshua set up a large stone as an additional reminder of their promise. This stone, he said, had also heard what was said and would stand as a testimony against those "untrue to your God."

Keeping your promises to your teammates and coaches in regard to training, for example, is very important. Never forget that.

But promises of loving obedience to your Lord are to be taken with *total* seriousness. He's the ultimate promise keeper, and He made us to be like Him.

In past years our team has occasionally held a meeting without me, when team members went around the table and asked their fellow players to hold them accountable, knowing they might need help from time to time. All of us need reminders.

One year our team's reminder was a witness stone. We had the custodial staff place a large stone in our locker room, a witness to the pledges we as a Christian team had made. Your mom probably wouldn't want such a big rock in your room, but have you ever thought about putting at least a fist-sized stone on your dresser, as a reminder of the promises you've made to Him?

Keep a cross nearby, too, perhaps as a beautiful, shiny symbol you wear around your neck, or maybe something as simple as two sticks lashed cross-wise on your wall, to remind you that when you pray for forgiveness for broken promises, you will most surely receive it through Christ our Lord, whom the New Testament also calls a stone, "the stone the builders rejected."

There's no better foundation in all the world than that stone and no more comforting presence than His presence.

CHALLENGES:

Do you need to be reminded of promises you once made but haven't fulfilled?

Would you have the courage to tell your friends what the stone on your dresser means, if they ask?

Who can you ask to help hold you accountable for your faith development?

WHOSE WILL BE DONE?

Thinking Back on Joshua's Life

Watching contract negotiations between professional teams and prospective players can be quite a spectacle. This past summer it was, among others, cornerback Darrelle Rivas of the New York Jets. Rivas wanted more; the Jets insisted on giving less than he was asking. The battle of wills went on late into the summer. And that's only one example, of course.

The world of professional sports is not the only place that sees such a battle of wills. It can go on in homes, as parents and their children sometimes lock horns. It happens in school, when a teacher's demands meet angry student resistance. It can even happen in church, when two different people or groups differ on some issue and both are convinced they're following God's will. It can occur on high school or middle school teams, when players (or their parents) disagree with a coach's decision.

Sometimes those battles may have a humorous aspect. Let's face it: We tend to look silly when we become stubborn. But often there's nothing funny about those clashes at all. People get hurt, sometimes badly. And the longer that battle of wills goes on, the worse the situation gets.

Joshua didn't have that problem in his relationship with God. No battle of wills there; he never objected to what the Lord said to him. He was a great military and political leader and a strong spiritual influence on the Israelites. No one would call him a pushover. But he knew that he had not been successful because he had rammed his own will through. Instead, he had all along the way submitted to what the Lord said. He was a living Old Testament example of someone who both lived and said, "Your will be done."

In athletics, as we've noted, communication, commitment, trust and involvement are vital to any team's health. But finally, when there are clashes, strong-willed individuals have to adjust to what is good for the group. And that can mean swallowing your pride, which often doesn't go down easily.

Submission to God's will, of course, is never negotiable. Graciously and wholeheartedly saying "yes" to His way and His Kingdom purposes is the only way to His kind of peace, hope, joy and success. We're called to make His will ours every day and in all we do, say and pray.

CHALLENGES:

Think of some clashes of wills that caused hurt and pain to you or to others.

Why can it be so hard to submit, to gracefully back down?

What are the benefits of backing down?

What do you really mean when you pray, "Your will be done"?

WINNERS AND LOSERS

Thinking Back on Joshua Again

A few years back, T-shirts with the slogan "The one who dies with the most toys wins" became popular. Is that what winning is all about—accumulating toys? And what are those toys anyway?

The answer to the last question is all around us and can threaten our Christian walk. Toys can be video games, boats, woodworking equipment, clothes and shoes, cars, jewelry, cruises, golf clubs, quilting equipment, tennis rackets, swimming pools or the homes we live in. And the list could go on forever.

None of those things obviously is wrong in itself, if it is used wisely and in obedience to the absolute priority of God's Kingdom. And if we remember in our hearts that it is finally only a thing, a toy, and if we don't allow it to become our master and block out the needs of our neighbor, or do harm to God's good creation.

Our culture values winning, too, especially in athletics. In sports, it often boils down to win-loss records, statistics and the ability to beat an archrival. The team that ends with the most points wins.

It follows, then, that in high school or middle school sports, a coach working with kids without great talent and with an unimpressive win record is seen as a loser, regardless. This happens even though she or he may get those kids to perform to the best of their ability, and even though that coach may teach young athletes wonderful things like how to lose, how to win, how to respect opponents, how to care for teammates and the like. Such coaches are still losers, as far as most fans are concerned.

The book of Joshua has a different take on winning. Winners are people who are strong and courageous, people who obey their Lord's commands gratefully, people who support one another, people who with His help clean the idols out of their lives. Winning a game is fun, but such Kingdom-oriented people set the real standard for winning. Mother Teresa put it this way: "It's not about success; it's about faithfulness."

In the New Testament the Apostle Paul says a curious thing as he looks back at his life. Instead of seeing winning the race as a sign of victory, he talks first about *finishing the course*, about living a life of obedience to God's way, a life of trust, faithfulness and commitment, all the way through, even until death itself.

Christians able to do that, by God's grace, will also joyously share in Christ's winning.

CHALLENGES:

What is your definition of winning? Of success?

Do you know any winners who never won a race or a game?

ENTHUSIASM

Thinking Back: Joshua and Paul

A re you enthusiastic about the sport you're in? Enthusiastic enough to carry you through training, low points after lost games, and tough practices when you and your team seem to be getting nowhere? I hope you are. Oliver Wendell Holmes, whom you may have met in American lit, once said, "Nothing great was ever achieved without enthusiasm."

Do you find it more fun to watch high school- or college-level games than the pros? Many people do. They feel that players on those levels show more enthusiasm than the pros do. But even in professional games it can be enjoyable to watch the eager, excited interaction between the players and the fans. Enthusiasm is fun to watch, fun to get caught up in.

How about the Christian life? Do you find it exciting and worthy of your enthusiasm or boring and ordinary? Is it something for timid people who don't know what life is really all about?

If it seems boring to you, you might do well to think about Joshua and all he went through, including spying in a strange land, crossing an impassible river, witnessing and participating in the fall of Jericho's walls, and fighting many fierce battles against numerically stronger forces. That was boring?

Or consider the Apostle Paul, who went through adventures without end in his life of faithful obedience to his Savior. He was flogged and beaten eight times, stoned once, shipwrecked three times and exposed to incredible danger. But through it all, his enthusiasm and excitement never wore thin. The word "boring" was not in his vocabulary.

An athletic season is naturally full of its own kind of excitement. There are trips, games, exuberant celebrations after victory, tight contests, and locker room talks and antics. There's the satisfaction of knowing you've bettered your personal record as a runner or your times in the freestyle. Excitement, enthusiasm and success all feed off one another.

Enthusiasm is a God-given gift. He gave you a healthy body and a heart that can get caught up in play, that can be enthusiastic and ready to roll. Enjoy the sports and the other activities He has given you! Have fun, and look forward to the next game. Cheer your teammates on in both good times and tough ones. Use every chance you have to praise the God who gave you these opportunities.

Enthusiasm is catching, whatever your activity. Pass it forward.

And be thankful to the God who makes it all possible.

CHALLENGES:

Do you find it hard to be enthusiastic when things go wrong in sports or other projects?

What opportunities in your Christian life are exciting?

If there aren't any such exciting opportunities, what do you think might be wrong?

GO FOR IT

Joshua 23

In 2005 Ryan Grant was an undrafted football player coming out of college who was signed not to be a regular player, but only to be on the New York Giants' practice team. When the Green Bay Packers traded for him in 2007, he was pretty much an unknown. However, in the fifth game of that season he got a chance to run the football, and over the next two and a half years he gained the second-most rushing yards of any player in the NFL. He surely didn't settle for being "ordinary."

As a coach, I'd never say to a team, "Let's go out and be average today." The Lord never suggested that to Joshua. He expected him to use every last ounce of talent, courage, toughness, determination, inspiration and commitment for His glory. And he did.

At the beginning of the book of Joshua, God told him to be strong and courageous. Near the end of his life Joshua reminded Israel's leaders what God had done for them. Joshua never claimed he had led Israel successfully on his own, but he surely did stand out, using the strength God gave him to go for it. Joshua was anything but ordinary. He went for it.

God doesn't guarantee us wins on the field or the ability to lead our team in scoring. Neither does He promise us good looks and wealth. But in all of life, He expects us to go all out for His glory and the benefit of others, to do our best.

God won't call us to occupy a foreign land, as He did Joshua. But we're all part of some kind of group, some team, whether it be in school, church, business, or in relationships with family and friends.

We might be blessed with gifts to be a bold leader, perhaps a leader working behind the scenes, or maybe a follower. He might have given us abilities to be a starter, or maybe a reserve. Whatever the case, God asks us to use our gifts for Him—in the highest fashion possible for us. He asks of you that you humbly make the most of whatever gifts you have been given in His service and to the glory of His name. He asks you to go for it—for His sake and the sake of the people around you.

CHALLENGES:

What talents do you feel God has given you? Please be honest with yourself.

How can you use your talents best for His glory? Think about it.

INDEX OF COMMON THEMES

APPENDIX 1:
CALVIN COLLEGE AND ATHLETICS

With approximately 4,000 students, Calvin is one of North America's largest and most respected Christian colleges. Calvin, founded in 1876, aims to provide a vigorous liberal arts education that promotes lifelong service. The college's outstanding faculty has earned worldwide respect for producing substantial and challenging art and scholarship. In addition, Calvin's reputation as a caring community is evidenced by a warm campus environment that develops the whole person.

Calvin faculty, students, staff and alumni live out the college's motto: "My heart I offer to you, Lord, promptly and sincerely."

Calvin's curriculum is shaped by the Christian faith as reflected in the Reformed creeds; because of the college's relatively large size, Calvin is able to offer a diverse, Christian liberal arts education. The curriculum features more than 100 majors and programs, numerous off-campus and foreign study programs, a five-floor library with more than 600,000 holdings, many support services and a beautiful 400-acre campus.

Calvin is a National Collegiate Athletic Association (NCAA) Division III institution, and as such it promotes the true student-athlete experience. The college offers 17 varsity sports and three club sports. As a Division III school, it does not award any athletic-based financial aid or scholarships. Athletes are students first, play for the love of the sport, are supported to pursue academic interests, and live in and among other Calvin students as friends and peers. Yet Calvin's excellence in the classroom is matched by success in athletics. Calvin has won nine NCAA Division III national team championships, including women's volleyball in 2010; men's basketball in 1992 and 2000; women's cross country in 1998 and 1999; and men's cross country in 2000, 2003, 2004 and 2006. In addition, 14 teams have finished as national runners-up.

Through the fall of 2010, Calvin has produced 87 College Sports Information Directors of America (CoSIDA) Academic All-Americans, which ranks in the top 10 of all NCAA III institutions. For the past 15 consecutive years, Calvin has posted a top-25 finish in the final NCAA III Learfield Sports Directors' Cup standings. The National Association of Collegiate Directors of Athletics and Learfield Sports present the cup annually to the best overall collegiate athletics programs in the country, based on points earned by teams that compete in NCAA Championship events. Calvin is one of only seven schools in the country to finish in the top 25 every year that the competition has been held at the NCAA III level.

Calvin has been a member of the Michigan Intercollegiate Athletic Association (MIAA) since the fall of 1953.

For more information, see *www.calvin.edu/sports*.

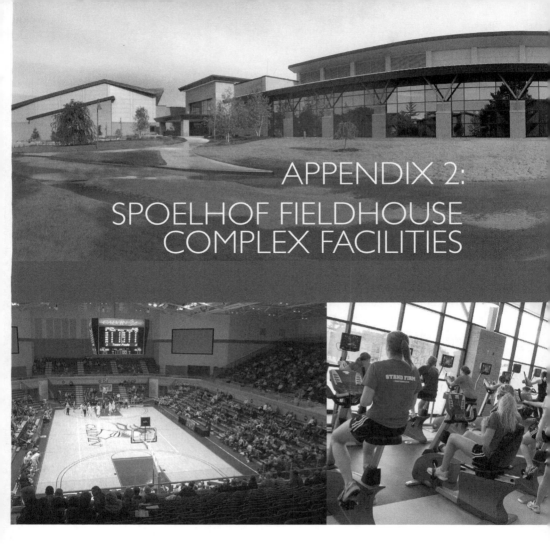

APPENDIX 2: SPOELHOF FIELDHOUSE COMPLEX FACILITIES

VAN NOORD ARENA

- Seats approximately 5,000 for major events
- Four full-sized basketball courts so that men and women, junior varsity and varsity, can practice concurrently
- Two weight room facilities; the athletic weight room for members of Calvin's 17 varsity teams is 8,000 square feet
- 10,000-square-feet fitness center for the general student body, faculty and staff
- Athletic training room provides state-of-the-art treatment and rehabilitation to student athletes
- 10 locker rooms for students and staff
- Two concession stands.

VENEMA AQUATIC CENTER

- Olympic-sized, 50-meter pool with moveable bulkheads accommodates multiple events at the same time

- Pool accommodates 22 lanes at 25 yards each for laps or racing

- Pool has 850,000-gallon capacity with high-tech filtration system

- Spectator seating capacity is 500

- Pool is 15 feet at diving end, 4 feet deep in the middle for swimming lessons and instruction, and 7 feet deep at the starting blocks

- Pool has four diving boards: two at 1 meter and two at 3 meter

- Includes a "wet classroom," where athletes can learn swimming and diving techniques immediately before and after entering the pool

HUIZENGA TENNIS & TRACK CENTER

- Multi-sport use: tennis, track, baseball, softball, volleyball
- Four full-sized tennis courts
- Sturrus 200-meter indoor track
  - Six race lanes
  - Eight straight-away lanes
  - Two sand pits
  - Competition and practice pole vault lanes

STRIKWERDA OUTDOOR TENNIS CENTER

- Six outdoor courts

HOOGENBOOM HEALTH & RECREATION CENTER

- Three full-sized courts for recreational basketball and volleyball
- Human performance lab
- Dance studio
- Health services department
- Five classrooms
- Locker rooms, equipment storage and laundry
- 38-foot-high by 80-foot-wide climbing wall
  - Simulated rock free-form surface inspired by Red River Gorge in Kentucky
  - 16 hanging ropes
  - Eight "splitter" cracks
  - More than 40 routes designed for a range of abilities
  - 50-foot diameter boulder